# FAMOUS SAMURAI

# FAMOUS SAMURAI
## The Two Courts Period

*An Illustrated Biography of Japan's Greatest Swordsmen*

# WILLIAM DE LANGE

For more on books by William de Lange visit:
**www.williamdelange.com**

First edition, 2017

Published by TOYO Press

Copyright © 2017 by William de Lange

Protected by copyright under the terms of the International Copyright Union; all rights reserved. Except for fair use in book reviews, no part of this book may be reproduced for any reason by any means, including any method of photographic reproduction, without the permission of the publisher.

ISBN 978-1-891640-94-0

Library of Congress Cataloging-in-Publication data available upon request.

# CONTENTS

Nenami Okuyama Jion            1

Chūjō Hyōgo no Kami Nagahide        79

Glossary            165

Index            167

# NENAMI JION

## Fujigatani Castle

What is it that propels a man to greatness? Is it the soil from which he is brought forth? Is it the circles in which he was raised? We may never know all the mysterious factors that combine to bring forth those who stand out from their fellow men. What is certain is that in the case of our protagonist all these factors played their own particular roles and ultimately combined to produce the greatest Japanese swordsman of the fourteenth century. His name was Nenami Jion, the first great fencing master whose name has come down to us through the mists of time. Only very little is known about the life and exploits of Jion himself, yet much is known about his background, for he was born in the mid-fourteenth century as Sōma Yoshimoto, scion of the powerful Sōma, a clan founded by Sōma Yoshikado, son of the great Taira no Masakado, who had subdued the realm's eastern provinces during the tenth century.

Yoshimoto's father, Sōma Tadashige, possessed a small estate near the village of Tobari, in the northern province of Shimōsa. The Sōma clan did well, especially after the turn of the thirteenth century, when Yoshimoto's father gradually widened the Sōma sphere of influence and built a castle in

# Famous Samurai: The Two Courts Period

*Opposite page*: Sōma Yoshikado *(left)*, founder of the Sōma clan

the village of Fujigatani, hidden away along the southern reaches of the Tega Marshes.

The main instrument in the success of Sōma Tadashige was his vassalage to the Nitta clan. Their leader, Nitta Yoshisada, was a powerful northern warlord who had his power base at Kanayama castle, just across the border with Kōzuke, near the village of Ōta. The Nittas were direct descendants of the Seiwa Genji, a branch of the Minamoto, and thus distant relatives of Minamoto Yoritomo. As such, the Nittas owed direct allegiance to the Bakufu, but Yoshisada had never been a keen vassal. During the Gempei War Yoshisada's ancestors had failed to rally to the side of the Minamoto. As a result the Nitta clan never enjoyed any prominent position at the Bakufu court in Kamakura. Instead, they had withdrawn to the north where they could be their own masters and await the right moment to wreak their revenge on the Hōjō and thereby restore the family fortunes. That moment

Nenami Okuyama Jion

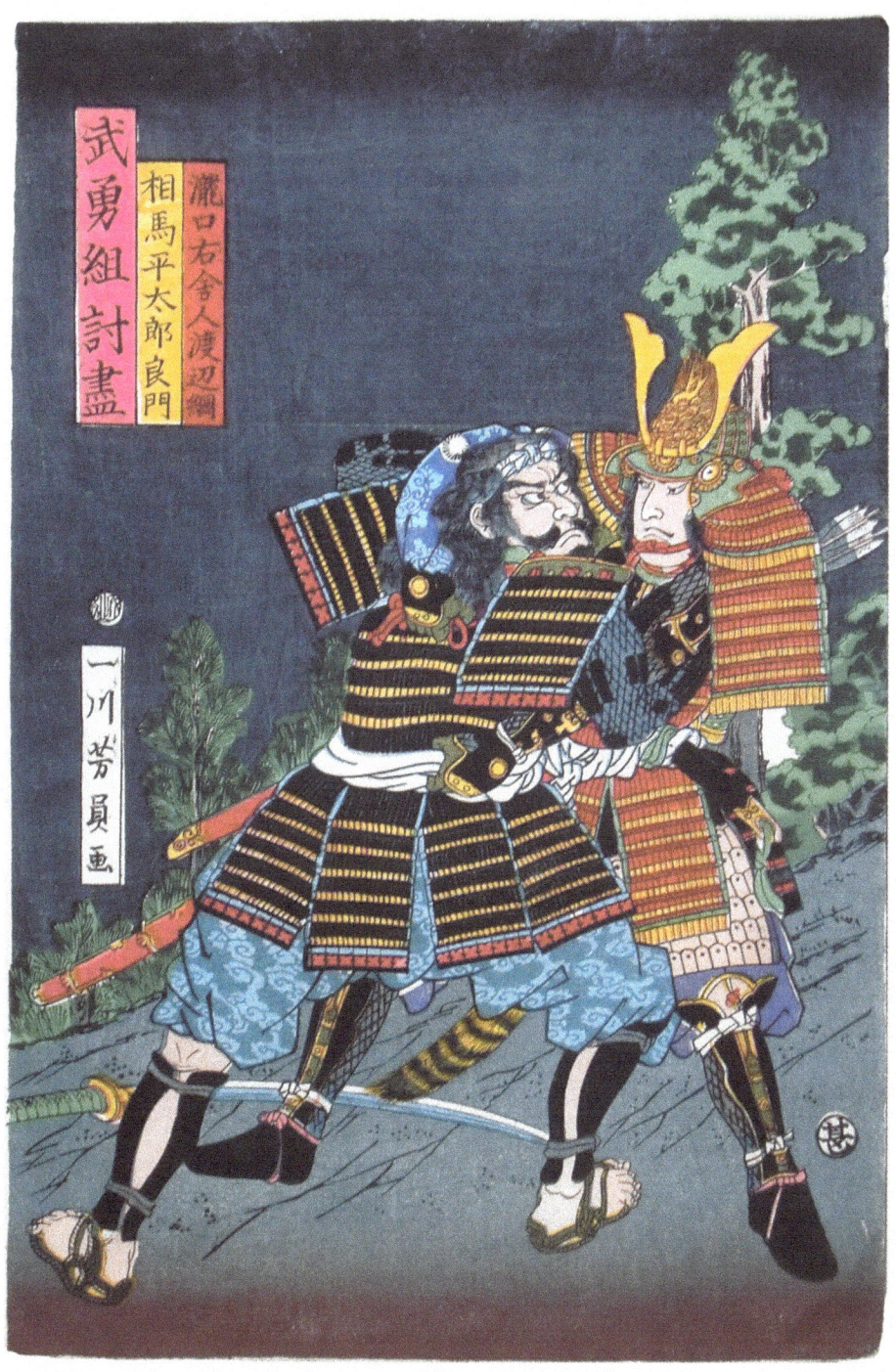

# Famous Samurai: The Two Courts Period

came in the spring of 1333, when word arrived in Kanayama castle that the exiled emperor Go-Daigo had managed to escape from the island of Oki and had landed on the main island of Honshū.

## Revolt

Few could have foreseen at that time that the flight of this lone figure, making his way to the Japanese mainland in the small boat of a local fisherman and covered in the cloak of a wandering monk, would set in motion a chain of events that would have immense and in so many ways tragic consequences, for the fortunes of the holders of small fiefdoms such as Sōma Tadashige, for the fortunes of his lord Nitta Yoshisada, and for the fate of the country as a whole.

Only two years earlier, Go-Daigo had still held court in the Kazan palace in Kyoto, acting out his role as the symbolic head of state. He was one of a long line of emperors that, according to Japan's historical mythology, went back all the way to the creation of the state of Yamato by the sun goddess Amaterasu Ō-Mikami. For many centuries the imperial house had ruled supreme over the small realm, which was then still mainly concentrated

Emperor Go-Daigo, who sought to restore power to the imperial throne

Yoshisada's rise to arms is still being celebrated today at the Ikushina shrine

around the Kyoto basin. In the course of the tenth century, partly through its own neglect, it went into decline. With that decline it was inevitable that political power was absorbed by rising provincial magnates. It happened to be the Fujiwara who were the most powerful magnates of the time and duly they took over the reigns of power. In their wisdom they chose not to depose of the emperor, but to appoint a regent through whose offices the emperor would be "guided" in his policies. In time, the Fujiwara, too, went into decline, but the example they had set was followed, as their military successors likewise chose to maintain the imperial throne as a symbolic force through which to bolster and legitimize their covert and de facto rule.

Something in the emperor had rebelled against this state of affairs. From the very start of his reign, in 1318, Go-Daigo had sought to restore to his throne the powers it had originally enjoyed. By 1331 he had come a long way in reaching his goal, but in that year his plot to overthrow the Bakufu was discovered by the then regent, Hōjō Takatoki. As the de facto leader of the Kamakura Bakufu, Takatoki held the real strings of power, and exercising those powers, he had sent Go-Daigo into exile to the island of Oki.

# Famous Samurai: The Two Courts Period

Nenami Okuyama Jion

*Opposite page*: Nitta and his warriors cross the Tone River

It was not long after the news of Go-Daigo's escape that Nitta Yoshisada received a missive from Go-Daigo to overthrow the Hōjō. Summoning all his vassals, Yoshisada raised his banner before the Ikushina shrine in his home province of Kōzuke. His first action was to eject the Bakufu's constable in his province. Then, on the evening of June 20, he ordered his men to cross the Tone River and march into Musashi. Their destination was the Miura Peninsula, at which western foot lay the center of Bakufu power, Kamakura.

No more than a hundred and fifty mounted warriors had joined Nitta Yoshisada when he set out from the Ikushina shrine. Among them were some of his staunchest vassals, Satomi Yoshitane, Ōdachi Muneuji, Horiguchi Sadamitsu, and of course, Yoshimoto's father, Sōma Tadashige, all men who were willing to give their life for the greater cause.

There were also those who had less faith in the successful outcome of their venture. They pointed out that the forces of Hōjō Takatoki were vastly superior to their own and suggested they throw up barricades behind the Tone River and await the help of allied warriors from the northeastern province of Echigo. The *Taiheiki* describes how Yoshisada's brother, Wakiya Yoshisuke, came forward and reminded his fellow warriors that:

> Those who follow the way of the bow and arrow have a duty to hold their name high and think light of death. The acting governor of Sagami [Hōjō Takatoki], whose house has ruled the realm for nigh on one hundred and sixty years, still exercises his might and his commands are not to be taken lightly. All the more so, we can not hope to defend ourselves by entrenching ourselves behind the Tone River if our luck has run out. And how can we rely on a clan from Echigo, if in the end we were to fall out and they to criticize our plan. How unbearable it would be if words like "this is the place to which this or that fellow fell back without any accomplishment or anything noteworthy to his name," or "a certain Nitta fled abroad and was struck down because he slayed a messenger from the governor of Sagami." If we take these lives—lives that will surely be lost on the field of battle—to offer them up on behalf of the imperial family, and declare ourselves rebels, our valor will bring honor to our descendants.

# Famous Samurai: The Two Courts Period

Fortune, that day, was indeed with Yoshisada and his men. No sooner had they crossed the Tone River, than they were joined by some two thousand warriors from the province of Echigo, forces of allied chieftains of the houses of Satomi, Toriyama, Tanaka, Ōida, and Hanekawa. When they pitched camp that night they were joined by five thousand more men, yet more warriors from the province of Echigo, but also from Kai and Shinano. Nor was this all, for on the next day a host of warriors from the provinces of Kōzuke, Shimotsuke, Kazusa, Hitachi, and Musashi also joined their ranks. So much had their ranks swollen by then, that "the Musashi plains, which stretch for more than eight hundred leagues in the four directions of the wind, were filled with their men and horses."

The first encounter between the rebel forces and those of the Bakufu came on June 23, on the plains of Kotesashi, when Yoshisada's forces were met by a large force under the command of Sakurada Sadakuni and Nagasaki Takashige. That day drew to a close without a victory for either of the two forces, but on the following day, Sadakuni's forces were routed. More encounters followed. The fiercest was on June 27 and 28, when a Bakufu force of some ten thousand troops under the command of Hōjō Yasuie engaged Yoshisada's forces in the river basin of the Tama River. On the first day of

Yoshisada clashes Takashige's forces at Kotesashi

# Nenami Okuyama Jion

The Tama River, Mount Fuji in the background

fighting, at a place called Bubaigawara, Yasuie managed to throw the invading forces back, yet he failed to follow up his initial victory, revelling instead in the triumphs of the day. That evening Yoshisada's forces were joined by those of Miura Yoshikatsu, a warlord from the Miura peninsula, who was well informed about the Hōjō movements and related to Yoshisada the complacency of Yasuie and his generals. Encouraged by Yoshikatsu's words Yoshisada regrouped his forces overnight and reopened the attack at a place called Sekido in the early dawn of the next morning. Taken utterly by surprise, Yasuie's forces were unable to stand their ground and were forced to retreat. Seizing the opportunity, Yoshisada crossed the Tama River and began to pursue the Bakufu's forces southward, toward the Kewai pass, the western gateway to the town of Kamakura.

There were seven main roads of entry through the surrounding hills and all of them were guarded by large Bakufu garrisons. Following his victory at

# Famous Samurai: The Two Courts Period

The temple town of Kamakura, headquarters of the Kamakura bakufu

Bubaigawara, Yoshisada had pursued Yasuie's forces along the Higher Kamakura Road, which followed an inland route, through the province of Sagami, toward Fujisawa. They reached the Kewai pass on the evening of July 1. Meanwhile, an allied force under the command of Chiba Sadatane and Oyama Hidetomo had marched on Kamakura following the Lower Kamakura Road, which skirted the coast of Edo bay. At Tsurumi, they had routed a large Bakufu force under the command Hōjō Sadamasa and, pressing on, they had reached the eastern outskirts of Kamakura roughly at the same time that Yoshisada had reached its western outskirts.

Both forces now held Kamakura as if in a vise, but still the Hōjō resisted. They split their forces into three large contingents, and intense fighting ensued at three of the seven approaches, at Kobukuro pass in the north, and at the passes at Kewai and the Gokuraku temple in the west. Horiguchi

# Nenami Okuyama Jion

Sadamitsu, who led the attack at Kobukuro pass had most success. After countless exchanges, his opponent Hōjō Moritoki, seeing that his forces were decimated, took his life, and with him so did most of his remaining warriors. Yoshisada, who led the attack at Kewai pass, was also making headway. But then word reached him that Ōdachi Muneuji, who led the attack at the Gokuraku temple, had fallen and that his troops were being driven westward, out of Kamakura, toward Koshigoe. On hearing this, Yoshisada quickly regrouped and led his men in a circular movement and began to approach Kamakura by following the coast until they reached Cape Inamura.

A fierce wind had been blowing for days, and high waves were pounding the coast. There was just no way they could pass the narrow beachhead that separated them from the town. Taking in the scene, Yoshisada walked up to the edge of an overhanging cliff and, beseeching the gods, cast his golden sword into the boiling sea below. As if by miracle, the winds began to lessen.

Yoshisada casts his golden sword into the sea at Cape Inamura

# Famous Samurai: The Two Courts Period

*Opposite page:* the ambitious general Ashikaga Takauji

They waited until the water had receded and that same day his troops crossed the head of the bay to pour into the town's streets from the undefended beach of Yuigahama.

For four more days, the Hōjō continued to hold out against Yoshisada's forces, but on the fourth day, on July 5, 1333, Takatoki, seeing that he was fighting a losing battle, ordered his men to set fire to the Bakufu buildings. That same day, Takatoki, thirty-four of his family members, and some two-hundred-and-eighty of their retainers withdrew to the Tōshō monastery and committed suicide en masse.

Thus the Kenmu Restoration, in which full power was restored to the throne was a feat. But Go-Daigo was not to rule for long, for not all of his warrior chieftains were as loyal as Nitta Yoshisada. There were other, more ambitious chieftains—men who were used to giving orders and thought that emperors should dedicate themselves to their ceremonial role, leave the serious task of governing the country to their generals.

## Ashikaga Takauji

One such ambitious chieftain was Ashikaga Takauji. His clan was one of the wealthiest in the east of Japan, and like the Nittas, directly descendant from the Seiwa Genji. Initially, Takauji had fought hard for Go-Daigo's cause. While Yoshisada had marched on Kamakura, Takauji had marched on Kyoto and destroyed the Bakufu strongholds in the imperial capital. But when, in the distribution of honors that followed, he was merely made governor of Musashi, he could hardly contain his resentment.

Given his high birth and given his contribution to a restoration of which he had hardly approved, he had expected to be appointed shōgun. In was in that capacity that, in the spring of 1335, he had hoped to lead a punitive expedition to Kamakura in order to suppress some remnant Hōjō forces there. His request was turned down, and when he had done his duty, he refused to return to Kyoto, even when Go-Daigo summoned him to do so. He had done so partly on the insistence of his brother, Tadayoshi, who, though a lesser general, was superior to his brother in intellect and political maneuvering.

Nenami Okuyama Jion

# Famous Samurai: The Two Courts Period

Thus Takauji took up residence in the compounds of the Eifuku monastery and set about building a grand palace at the former sight of the Minamoto headquarters.

The first real sign that Takauji was intent on usurping power came on December 16, 1335, when his brother, Tadayoshi, sent out word to warriors throughout the country that "Nitta Yoshisada must be destroyed" and that they were to assemble their clansmen and hasten to join him. To counter the threat, the imperial court issued a message to the opposite effect, and commissioned Yoshisada to orchestrate the destruction of the rebel forces. The messages sent shockwaves throughout the country. Warlords in each and every corner of every province began to consider their positions. Those closest to the fire, in the Kantō and around the capital, were forced to choose sides immediately, as a failure to do so would inevitably lead to their destruction. Before long, two great forces were marching toward each other along the Tōkaido, one eastward under the command of Yoshisada, the other westward under the command of one of Takauji's generals, Kō Moroyasu. On January 8, 1336, the two armies reached the Yahagi River in the province of Mikawa. The first showdown came shortly afterwards, when Yoshisada's forces crossed the river and pressed Takauji's forces all the way back to the province of Suruga, where, at a place called Tegoshigawara, Moroyasu's troops managed to maintain a precarious stand.

It seems that at this point Takauji was in the hold of conflicting emotions. Perhaps he was racked by guilt over the course he had taken, for he withdrew to the Jōkōmyō temple for quiet contemplation. In his stead, his brother rode out to Tegoshigawara at the head of a few thousand men to take charge of the fighting. But on January 18, in another fierce battle, Tadayoshi was forced to withdraw into the mountains of Hakone—he and his men had been driven back to within only twenty miles of Kamakura.

Only then, when his brother's life was in peril, did Takauji act. Assembling another large force, he set out westward along the Tōkaidō and, on January 24, pitched camp at a hamlet by the name of Takenoshita. Heavy fighting ensued the next day, but this time the roles were reversed when two of Yoshisada's allies defected to Takauji's side. Over the next few weeks, while Yoshisada's forces fell back along the Tōkaidō toward the west, Takauji's

forces continued to grow, as one warlord after another decided to join the rebellious forces. Retreating before this overwhelming force, Yoshisada's men were forced to fall all the way back to Kyoto. There, in the course of three days of intense fighting, between the 19th and 22nd of February 1336, they suffered a stunning defeat. Go-Daigo was forced to seek refuge at the Enryakuji, one of the monasteries of the powerful and Loyalist Tendai sect on Mount Hiei.

Takauji had won the battle, but by no means had he won the war. No sooner had he installed himself in Kyoto than news arrived that new Loyalist forces were closing in on the capital. The largest, some fifty thousand men, were under the command of Kitabatake Akiie.

Though only eighteen years old, Akiie was fully up to the task, for men of the Kitabatake clan were a force to be reckoned with. His father, Kitabatake Chikafusa, was one of Go-Daigo's closest advisers and the chief strate-

# Famous Samurai: The Two Courts Period

gist behind the Loyalist campaign. The Kitabatake were courtiers of noble birth. Like the Nitta and the Ashikaga, they, too, descended from the Genji, but theirs was the far more distinguished Murakami branch. Following the overthrow of the Hōjō, Akiie had been appointed governor of the northern province of Mutsu, where he had made Taga castle his headquarters. It was there, some five hundred miles from the capital, that he had raised an army. He had pressed his men hard to catch up with Takauji's advance from Kamakura, and the effort had paid off, for by February 25, only two days after his enemy had claimed victory, Akiie's troops crossed Lake Biwa to join the emperor at Mount Hiezan.

Encouraged by the arrival of reinforcements, Yoshisada's troops, which had been driven out of the capital, regrouped and engaged Takauji's troops

Kitabatake Akiie, son of the chief strategist behind the campaign of the Loyalists

with renewed vigor. During the first clashes that followed, Takauji's chief commander was routed and after three days of tough fighting it was Takauji who was forced to evacuate the capital. Pursued relentlessly by Yoshisada's troops, he retreated westward, to the province of Tamba, from where, after a last stand on the shores of the Inland Sea, he embarked with his troops and set sail for the southern island of Kyushu.

Now it was the turn of the Loyalists to claim victory, and they did so with great fervor. For weeks the capital was immersed in festivities, as its citizens, weary of the constant fighting in and around the capital over the previous year, revelled in their new-found liberty. Kitabatake Akiie was hailed by all as the hero of the day and laden with military honors by the court. Yoshisada, meanwhile, frustrated by his failure to destroy his enemy, sought diversion in the delightful attentions of his paramour at court, the beautiful Kōtō no Naishi. All seemed intoxicated by the rush of victory and only few alert to the lurking dangers—the long road that had to be completed before the Bakufu forces were fully routed. One of the few was Kusunoki Masashige, an unselfish Loyalist who hailed from the province of Kawachi. Masashige was highly and widely esteemed, both for his valor and his breadth of learning. His greatest gift was perhaps his foresight. He kept warning Go-Daigo that any celebrations were overly premature, that Takauji was bound to return, and that, with every day that they failed to act, their chances for ultimate success were dwindling.

# The Final Showdown

It was partly on Masashige's insistence that the Loyalists at last sought to prepare the ground for the final showdown that must inevitably come and to suppress the remaining Bakufu sympathizers, both in the Kantō and in the so-called Home Provinces, the five provinces of Yamato, Yamashiro, Kawachi, Izumi, and Settsu, which were situated near the capital. Toward the end of April, Nitta Yoshisada marched into Harima province at the head of some sixty thousand troops. Soon he was confronted by a force under the command of Akamatsu Norimura, a powerful ally of the Bakufu. A few months earlier

# Famous Samurai: The Two Courts Period

Norimura had assisted Takauji in his retreat to Kyushu by holding down Yoshisada's forces at Tamba. This time round, however, his men were vastly outnumbered. After a brief stand his defenses crumbled and he had to retreat to the safety of Shirohata castle, situated in the west of the province.

Yoshisada now divided his troops into four legions. One, under the command of Ooida Ujitsune, was sent on to capture Fukuyama castle and thus provide a first defense in case Takauji returned from Kyushu over land. Another, under the command of Yoshisada's brother, Wakiya Yoshisuke, was sent across the border, into Bizen, to lay siege to Mitsuishi castle, the stronghold of Ishibashi Kazuyoshi, another staunch ally of Takauji. A third legion, under the command of Eda Yukiyoshi, was also sent across the border in order to assault a number of other strongholds. Yoshisada himself pursued the Akamatsu forces to Shirohata castle. Stubbornly defended, the castle failed to fall and the siege dragged on for weeks without any sign of success.

Then, toward the end of June, word arrived in the Nitta camp that, on the evening of June 14, Takauji had landed with an immense fleet at Tomo Bay in the province of Bingo, some sixty miles west along the coast from Shirohata castle. According to the informant the Ashikaga forces had remained there for five days. On the fifth day, half of the force had begun to march eastward under the command of Takauji's brother, Tadayoshi. The rest, including Takauji himself, had reembarked and set sail again, apparently also heading eastward. With no end of the siege in sight, and not knowing where Takauji intended to land, Yoshisada could do little else than end the siege and retreat eastward, sufficiently close to the capital to intercept both Tadayoshi's advance over land and Takauji's advance over sea.

Kitabatake Akiie, meanwhile, had marched east in the hope of crushing what remained of the Bakufu forces in Kamakura. He had more success than his fellow chieftain at Shirohata castle. Soon he had rallied a large number of northern allies, warlords from Mutsu and Hitachi, who were sympathetic to Go-Daigo's cause and feared a crushing overlordship from Kamakura. Together they decisively routed the Bakufu forces who engaged them at the banks of the Katase River, only a few miles west of Kamakura. The Bakufu forces, under the command of Shiba Ienaga, received another pounding and had to withdraw to Kamakura, leaving a number of their allies to their fate. Akiie now drove northward, toward the Kantō plain, where he took up residence in Utsunomiya castle and, with the help of local Loyalists, began to attack Bakufu allies in Shimotsuke and Mutsu. For the time being, the Bakufu forces in the east of the country did not pose a serious threat. The future of the country and the court by which it was to be ruled hinged on the outcome of the fight between the forces of Nitta Yoshisada and Ashikaga Takeuji.

Yoshisada's informant had been accurate enough in his description of Takauji and Tadayoshi's movements. Having parted with Takauji, Tadayoshi had immediately headed for Fukuyama castle. He had completely surprised the forces of Ooida Ujitsune, which had as yet failed to reduce the castle and now fled before the onslaught. Ujitsune led them eastward, toward Mitsuishi castle, in an effort to unite them with those of Wakiya Yoshisuke and thus halt the onslaught. In his first objective he succeeded, but such was the force and the pace of Tadayoshi's army that only by making a united front

# Famous Samurai: The Two Courts Period

did Yoshisada's troops stand a chance of halting them. At length, all of the Loyalist legions managed to regroup. They converged on a stretch of land along the Minume Bay, set off to the west by the Minato River and to the east by the Ikuta River. There, some ten miles west of Osaka, between the points where the Minato and Ikuta rivers poured themselves into the Inland Sea, they set up their defenses and awaited the combined assault of the two Ashikaga brothers.

That assault came on July 4, 1336. The first success of the day went to the Loyalists, who managed to repel Takauji's fleet when it attempted to land and form a beachhead between the two rivers, in the thick of Yoshisada's forces. Takauji's troops suffered heavy casualties, and only with great difficulty were they able to reembark and return to sea.

Yet it was only a temporary reprieve. From his high vantage point on the promontory of Cape Wada, Yoshisada observed with growing disquiet how Takauji's ships sailed farther eastward and made ready to land upon the undefended shores beyond the Ikuta River. At this point his nerves failed him. Already his troops were hard pressed by a vanguard of some two thousand of Tadayoshi's mounted warriors which had rapidly advanced along the shoreline from the west. Fearing to be locked in by a second assault from the east by

Takauji's fleet arrives in Mimune Bay

# Nenami Okuyama Jion

The Battle of Minatogawa is in full swing

Takauji, Yoshisada ordered his troops to withdraw eastward, across the Ikuta River, so as to secure his retreat and intercept the seaborne assault.

It was a fateful mistake. Not only did Yoshisada's troops fail to deflect the second landing; by ordering the withdrawal of his troops, he had left one of his main allies, Kusunoki Masashige, to bear the brunt of Tadayoshi's assault. Summoned at the last minute to come to Yoshisada's rescue, Masashige had taken up positions along the western banks of the Minato River. For six hours he and his men fought off Tadayoshi's superior forces. They were fighting a lost battle. At the end of the day, Masashige and some seven hundred of his retainers lay scattered along the dried-up riverbed, their noble blood staining brown the hot pebbles on that bright summer day.

By offering his life, Masashige had done nothing less than expiate Yoshisada's failure, a failure that could have been avoided had his wise counsel only been heeded earlier. It was an act of unselfish loyalty seldom seen in the annals of the gruesome years that were to follow, and one that earned him the undiminished admiration of warriors ever after.

Now the same dreadful and demoralizing pattern of the year before repeated itself, as once again the Loyalists were forced to fall back to Kyoto, and once again Go-Daigo had to take refuge in the monasteries on Mount

# Famous Samurai: The Two Courts Period

Hiei. Having only barely managed to extricate himself from the battlefield, Yoshisada set up camp at the foot of the mountain. Takauji and his brother, meanwhile, entered Kyoto in triumph. Many more exchanges followed over the following months, and though none of them resulted in a decisive victory for either party, from now on the fortunes of war invariably seemed to go against the Loyalists.

A great blow to the Loyalist cause came toward the end of that year, on November 13, when Go-Daigo chose to go over to Takauji's side. Having observed how Yoshisada's forces had been driven apart, and fearing for his position, Go-Daigo let himself be persuaded to come down the mountain and to return to the Kazan palace in order to resume his place as Japan's (symbolic) head of state. For a man who had aspired to rule, it was a coming-down in more than a literal sense. His humiliation was complete when the already demeaning settlement proved to be no more than a ruse, for no sooner did he arrive in Kyoto, than he was placed under house arrest.

Early in 1337 Go-Daigo managed to escape from captivity once again. This time he fled to the small village of Anou, hidden away among the Yoshino Mountains, a large tract of wild and mountainous country in the southern

Go-Daigo makes his escape toward the Yoshino Mountains

part of Yamato province. There, still refusing to accept defeat and assured of the continued support of Nitta Yoshisada and the other Loyalists, he set up a new court from which he was to lead repeated attempts to regain power.

Takauji, meanwhile, had founded a new military government. With the old headquarters in Kamakura destroyed, he founded a new Bakufu in the capital's Muromachi district, not far from the imperial palace. To placate hostile warlords, he ordered that the estates which had been confiscated in the wake of the Kenmu Restoration be returned to their former owners. On September 20, 1336, to give renewed legitimacy to the new Bakufu, he installed a member of another branch of the imperial family, Kōmyō, as puppet emperor on the throne in Kyoto.

From then on, and for the first time in Japanese history, the country had two courts, a Southern Court in Anou and a Northern Court in Kyoto. Both courts claimed imperial legitimacy, and for the remaining half of the fourteenth century the representative forces of both courts were to vie with each other for true military power.

## Escorting the Crown Prince

Sōma Tadashige continued to serve the Loyalist cause. Following the Kenmu Restoration he had been appointed to the Musha Dokoro, the Board of Warriors. This office, which was led by Nitta Yoshisada, had been set up shortly after Go-Daigo's return to Kyoto, and was responsible for keeping order among the warriors who were stationed in the capital. Apart from Tadashige it had some sixty-three officers on its payroll. After Takauji's revolt, Tadashige joined his lord on his many campaigns against the Ashikaga forces. He had been among the men who had crossed Yahagi River and pursued Takauji's forces all the way to the Hakone Pass. He had joined Yoshisada in the siege of Shirohata castle, had grappled with Takauji's forces on the shores of the Inland Sea, and again, at the foot of Mount Hiei. The *Taiheiki* describes how:

On the morning of August the twenty-fourth, at roughly eight o-clock, a large force of twenty thousand mounted soldiers, led by some five

# Famous Samurai: The Two Courts Period

*Opposite page:* Tsuruga, on the Japan Sea

hundred men from the governor of Kumano, came charging forward. Two famous master archers among the Loyalists, Honma Magojirō and Sōma Jirōzaemon [Tadashige], were seated in front of Yoshisada, and, looking down on the approaching men from Kumano, they quietly rose from their seats and, laughing loudly, said to each other "today the soldiers of our army need not draw any long swords, nor do they need to let fly any arrows. Let us advance and crush the skulls of these wretches." Then they drew their long-bows and fixed arrows of fifteen thumbs long to their bowstrings and Honma shot down a wild and strong warrior from among the enemy forces who approached them from the center, and next Sōma shot and mortally wounded a large warrior who looked like the gods who guards the entrance of a shrine. When the five hundred strong force of Kumano saw this they could neither advance nor retreat but all cowered. At length Honma and Sōma declared their names unto the enemy and challenged them, yet none of the twenty thousand mounted warriors sought to pursue them but vied with each other to be the first to retreat.

After the Loyalists were forced to relinquish the capital, Tadashige continued to follow his lord in battle. These years, as the indefatigable Yoshisada moved around the country, raising troops here and winning new allies in an effort to blow new life into the Loyalist campaign, were some of the hardest of Tadashige's life.

On November 13 (on the same day that Go-Daigo left for the capital) Tadashige joined Yoshisada, his brother Wakiya Yoshisuke, and some seven thousand Loyalist troops as they crossed Lake Biwa. They had been entrusted by Go-Daigo with the escort of Go-Daigo's sons, Crown Prince Tsunenaga and his brother Takanaga. They were to take them to Tsuruga, an important sea port on the Japan Sea, some ten miles north of Lake Biwa. Tsuruga lay in the predominantly Loyalist province of Echizen and had of old enjoyed close connections with the imperial court. They intended to take the shortest route, along the highroad that cut straight across the Nosaka Mountains.

All went well during the first leg of the journey. But at Shiozu they ran into a large force under the command of Shiba Takatsune, the Bakufu con-

Nenami Okuyama Jion

stable of Echizen, whose brother, Ienaga, had fallen in the defense of Kamakura. Takatsune had been warned of their advance and had ridden out from Echizen to block the roads toward Tsuruga. Greatly outnumbered, and unwilling to endanger the lives of their royal consorts, Yoshisada and his men were forced to make an eastern detour, along the Hokkoku Kaidō through Echizen. By now it was already late in November and among Japan's eastern mountains, exposed as they were to the cold winds from China, winter had set in fully. Struggling through deep snow in blistering winds, the battle-weary men managed to cross the Tochi no Ki and Ki no Me Passes only at the cost of extreme hardships. Finally, yet utterly exhausted, they reached the safety of Kanagasaki castle.

## Kanegasaki Castle

Situated on a rocky promontory overlooking Tsuruga bay, the castle of Kanagasaki was a formidable stronghold. On its eastern, northern and southern sides, steep walls dropped straight down into the sea. The only means of access to the castle over land was a long a narrow road along the promontory. The castle had only recently been built by the Echizen Loyalist Kehi Ujiharu. Thus far it had not seen much action, but with Yoshisada's arrival this was to change drastically. No sooner had he arrived than he began to raise levies and to contact local Loyalists to commit troops to a renewed attempt to regain the capital.

As soon as word arrived in Kyoto that Yoshisada had safely reached Tsuruga, Takauji sent word to his constables throughout the country to immediately march on Tsuruga and assist Shiba Takatsune in reducing Kanagasaki castle. By the time the first troops arrived in Tsuruga, Takatsune had already launched a number of fierce attacks on the stronghold, but to little effect and, in spite of the reinforcements, Takatsune was not at ease. His spies back home informed him that Wakiya Yoshisuke had persuaded the Bakufu ally Uryū Tamotsu to turn color and join the Loyalist cause. Tamotsu was the lord of Somoyama castle, situated some ten miles north-east of Tsuruga. Together they had raised a large army and signs were that they were about to march on Tsuruga at any moment. Kō Moroyasu, the Bakufu general who had been routed by Yoshisada at Yahagi River, was sent to Somoyama to intercept and destroy the pending threat. After a forced march of several days in the depth of winter, he reached Yu no O, a small hamlet at the foot of Mount Somo. His men were utterly exhausted, and to get them fit for battle Moroyasu ordered them to turn in for the night. Rested, they would surprise Uryū's forces at the break of dawn. It was a fatal mistake. News of their arrival had already reached the castle, and that night Tamotsu's men, their horses' hoofs wrapped with cloth, came down from the castle and raided the village. Moroyasu managed to escape with his life, but his men were decimated.

# Famous Samurai: The Two Courts Period

While Wakiya Yoshisuke returned to Tsuruga to relieve his brother, Tamotsu, emboldened by their recent victory, marched northward, on Shinzenkōji castle. This castle, which was situated at the center of the Takefu Basin, guarded the gateway to Echizen and thus formed the first line of defense for Kuromaru castle, the Shiba headquarters in the more northern town of Fukui. Only a few weeks earlier, Takatsune himself had taken the stronghold for the very purpose of providing a shield against Loyalist insurgents. Having been mobilized by Takauji to intercept Yoshisada on his way to Tsuruga, Takatsune had left behind only a skeleton force to man the castle. It fell within a few days.

In Tsuruga, meanwhile, those within Kanagasaki castle were still holding out. It had been late in November that Shiba Takatsune, having failed to intercept Yoshisada's troops, had reached Tsuruga and had taken up positions in front of the castle's forbidding walls. And it was one month into the siege, when Yoshisuke returned from Somoyama castle at the head of a few thousand mounted warriors. They took Takatsune's troops completely by surprise, breaking through their ranks and causing great havoc among them. Those inside the castle were greatly heartened at the sight of the Nitta banner. Some eight hundred men stormed out of the castle to join in the melee and claim the first triumph in the battle of Kanagasaki castle. Sadly, that triumph was their only one. They had only momentarily managed to break the siege, and though it had enabled Yoshisuke and his men to join those in the castle, their combined fighting power was not sufficient to lift the siege, and no more sorties were made from the fortress.

The first great blow to the fortunes of the now reunited brothers came when word reached the castle by sea that a second relief party, under the command of Uryū Tamotsu and the Loyalist chieftain Satomi Yoshiuji had been defeated. Having reduced Shinzenkōji castle, Uryū Tamotsu had joined forces with Yoshiuji and marched on Tsuruga at the head of a force of some five thousand men. But they were too late. Having heard of Takatsune's failure in fending off Yoshisuke's relief party, Takauji had raised yet another large force, so that by the time Tamotsu and his ally had set out from Shinzenkōji castle, the number of Bakufu troops that had converged on Tsuruga was close to sixty thousand. The two generals advanced right up to Hawara, a wide plain on the town's southern outskirts, when they were confronted by a force four times their size under the command of the Bakufu commander Imagawa Yorisada. They were utterly routed. Only a small number safely returned to Somoyama castle. The rest, including Satomi Yoshiuji and Uryū Tamotsu, laid down their lives on the snow-covered plains of Hawara.

As the weeks dragged on, the outlook for those within Kanagasaki castle began to look bleaker and bleaker. The *Taiheiki*, that epic account of the struggle between the Northern and Southern Courts, carries a powerful description of the dire state of those within the castle after two months of siege:

> As their rations dwindled with every day, the men sought to alleviate their hunger by catching the fish that entered the bay, and lived from day to day by collecting seaweed from the rocks. By these means they were able to stretch their lives a little and continue the fight. Yet as their plight worsened they were forced to turn even on their treasured horses that could still stand, first the horses of the troops and eventually even those that carried the generals; each day one was killed to be given to the men to eat at dawn and dusk.

The loyalists do battle with Bakufu troops

# Famous Samurai: The Two Courts Period

Today, only a memorial stone marks the place of Kanegasaki castle

It was a potent sign of their plight, for the eating of horse meat ran against their Buddhist beliefs. It also marked an irreversible turning point in the fortunes of Yoshisada's men, for in offering their horses they also gave up their last chance of breaking the siege. By the third month the conditions within the castle were so desperate that even the flesh of those who had fallen was not shunned. Three more weeks they held out, fighting off fierce and unrelenting assaults by day and by night, until finally, on April 7, their spirit broke. That day, at the break of dawn, Takauji's forces broke down the castle's wooden gate and killed all who still had life in them. Yoshisada's son, Yoshiaki, Kehi Ujiharu, as well as Crown prince Takanaga took their own lives. Crown prince Tsunenaga escaped in the confusion but was eventually captured on his way to Somoyama castle. He was taken to Kyoto where he was poisoned by Takauji's henchmen.

## Escape

Yoshisada, however, was not to be found. Ten days before the castle had fallen, he, his brother, and a number of his officers, including Tadashige, had escaped from Kanagasaki castle. They had slipped away by boat under the cloak of darkness to make land farther north along the coast, from where they reached Somoyama castle by foot.

The plight of the Loyalist cause, by now, was desperate. Kanagasaki castle seemed lost and there was little hope that Yoshisada and his brother could raise troops sufficiently in time to relieve his besieged men. Only few of the men who had rode out from Somoyama with Uryū Tamotsu the month before had returned alive. Besides Tamotsu, fifty-three of his men had died in action, while some five hundred had been seriously wounded. Of the chieftains only Wakiya Yoshisuke's son, Yoshiharu, who had been with them when they laid down their lives on the plains of Hawara had returned alive.

It was at this juncture that the account of Tamotsu's grieving widow poured new hope into the hears of the dejected warriors. Yoshiharu related to his father and uncle how the grief-stricken woman, taking in the cries of lament and self-reproach of her three surviving sons, had moved over to their side and addressed them, saying:

> You who headed toward Tsuruga, may have lost master Satomi through your negligence. Surely this is deeply regrettable. Yet how much more pitiful had it been if our lord and his brothers had returned safely having witnessed his death, for I would have had no words with which to console them. But knowing that your father, uncle, and his eldest son, all three died side by side with master Satomi [Yoshiuji] and that my remaining three sons will live on to serve our great commander is a source of the deepest consolation amidst my grief. Were I to lose in battle a thousand sons thinking first and foremost of their master I would have cause for neither anguish nor grief.

As she spoke these words she had poured out sake to reinvigorate the dejected Loyalist soldiers, even as the tears were running down her face.

## Famous Samurai: The Two Courts Period

Inspired by the widow's courage in her hour of despair, Yoshisada and his brother set about to assemble yet another force to relieve Kanegasaki castle, but they were unable to do so in time and forced to anxiously await the news of the fate of those whom they had left behind. That news reached them toward the middle of April, when they learned that all those whom they had left behind in the castle, including Yoshisada's son, Yoshiaki, were dead.

Though shaken to the core by this devastating, Yoshisada refused to admit defeat. By now he had learned of Go-Daigo's escape and the establishment of a second, Southern Court. And thus he decided to bide his time, spending the rest of the year in the rallying of new and not yet battle-weary troops among the many branches of the Nitta clan that had settled in the northern province of Echigo.

By April 1338 Yoshisada had once more assembled a formidable force. It was a year since Kanegasaki had fallen and his main opponent then, Shiba Takatsune, had meanwhile ensconced himself in Fuchū castle, situated in the

The former site of Somoyama castle

Only Fuchū castle's imposing main gate has survived the ages

small town of Takefu, less than fifteen miles north of Somoyama castle. Though a relatively small castle, given its strategic position at the center of Echizen, the Bakufu had made it their seat of power in the province. Takatsune had done so on Takauji's specific instructions, for though Kanagasaki had fallen, Takauji sensed that Yoshisada was far from defeated. In this he was right, for no sooner had the snow on the slopes of Mount Somo dissolved than Wakiya Yoshisuke marched northward at the head of some three thousand men to lay siege to the Bakufu stronghold. This time it was Takatsune who was outnumbered. Taking no chances, he abandoned the poor defenses of Fuchū castle and beat a retreat to Fukui, to the safety of Kuromaru castle. From there he sent out an urgent request to the Bakufu for reinforcements, built defenses across the plain, and awaited the inevitable assault that must follow.

# Famous Samurai: The Two Courts Period

## Nenami Okuyama Jion

Not long after he had moved to Kuromaru castle Takatsune was approached by the abbot of the Heisen monastery in Katsuyama, some fifteen miles east of Fukui. Like the Enryaku monastery on Mount Hiei, the Heisen monastery belonged to the Tendai sect, which had hitherto been on the side of the Loyalists. Of old, however, there had been a bone of contention between the two temples, as both laid claim to the Fujishima shrine, which stood on the southern banks of the Asuwa River. With Takatsune's ascendancy in Echizen, the abbot seized the opportunity to settle the matter for once and for all and offered him his monastery's support in exchange for the coveted shrine. This was no hollow offer. The Tendai was a powerful sect. It had at its disposal a large contingent of warrior monks, the notorious *sōhei*, who had proven their mettle while fighting on the side of the Loyalists at Mount Hiei. Takatsune readily agreed. On his request a large number of the *sōhei*, some five hundred in all, took up their station in Fujishima castle, which stood guard over the eponymous shrine and was one of the seven makeshift strongholds erected to halt Yoshisada's pending advance.

All positions were taken, then, when, toward the end of July 1338, Nitta Yoshisada sent out word to his troops and those of his allies to set up camp on the plains of Asuwa, not far from Fujishima castle. This time round the odds were firmly on the side of the Loyalists. As many as thirty thousand of them had gathered around the Nitta banner to deal the final and decisive blow to Takatsune's forces.

For Yoshisada, the act of betrayal on the part of the Tendai monks was of little significance in numerical terms, even though the seasoned warrior knew all too well that it took only a small and dedicated force to defend a stronghold. Yet there was for him another, more significant reason why he was troubled by the presence of the Tendai monks. The very shrine over which Fujishima castle stood guard was the family shrine of the Nitta house, and to Yoshisada, the Bakufu banner that now flew over the castle and its environs presented a spiritual menace. The experienced commander managed to hide these feelings from his men, but his horse must have sensed its master's unease, for on the point of their departure, it began to buck—a sight at which the tough and battle-hardened yet deeply superstitious men were overcome by a sense of foreboding.

*Opposite page*: Heisen temple, whose monks proved a serious threat to the Loyalists

# Famous Samurai: The Two Courts Period

Perhaps it was to dispel such haunting sentiments that Yoshisada reassembled his troops at Tōmyōji, situated east of Kuromaru castle, along he southern bank of the Kuzuryū River. There he once more raised his banner and divided his troops into seven regiments. Each regiment was to lay siege of one of Takatsune's seven strongholds by erecting *mukaijō*, makeshift strongholds that faced the existing strongholds and isolated them from others. Yet despite the equally makeshift nature of Takatsune's defenses, the Loyalists made little progress and the day drew to a close without any signs that any of the strongholds were about to surrender. As if to remind Yoshisada of their symbolic role, it was his former allies, the *sōhei* of the Tendai sect, who offered the fiercest resistance from Fujishima castle.

And it was then, as the summer sun began to set over Tsuruga Bay, and the landscape was immersed in a melancholic crimson glow, that fate took a hand. Yoshisada had remained behind at Tōmyōji to conduct the battle, but when he heard of the trouble his men were having with the tenacious *sōhei*, he selected some fifty cavalrymen and rode out to Fujishima castle to conduct the siege in person. It was an ill-timed decision. At the very moment at which Yoshisada and his men set out from Tōmyōji, a contingent of some three hundred mounted archers under the command of the Bakufu generals Hosokawa Takamoto and Kakusa Kimisuke left the gates of Kuromaru castle to come to the rescue of the besieged monks. By sheer chance both parties ran headlong into each other. The ensuing events are described in dramatic detail in the *Taiheiki*:

> Among Hosokawa's men there were many archers with shields, who ran into the wet rice fields, set up their shields in a row, and from behind them began to fire their arrows mercilessly; yet among Yoshisada's men there was not even one archer, nor had they any shields, so the soldiers formed a human shield so as to protect Yoshisada from the hail of arrows. "For a minor enemy we need no help from a great general" said Nakano Fujiuchisaemon, exchanging glances with Yoshisada, but Yoshisada would not hear of it and, with the words "I will not run alone from danger when I am losing men in great numbers," gave his horse the whip and drove in among the

# Nenami Okuyama Jion

enemy. Now his horse, a thoroughbred, capable of leaping across a moat of twelve feet with ease, was flinching at the arrows, having been hit by as many as five, and was unable to even cross a small ditch and tumbled down a precipice as if a folding screen had collapsed. At this point Yoshisada's left foot was caught and just when he tried to get up an arrow with white feathers hit the front of his helmet and caught him right between the eyes. Aware that the arrow had struck home, Yoshisada faltered as he felt darkness descend, and when he realized that his moment had come he passed his drawn long sword into his left hand and committed suicide amidst the deep mud by cutting off his own head, onto which his body collapsed.

The great Loyalist leader meets his end

With Yoshisada's death, the campaign had lost its momentum. one by one the assembled forces dispersed to return to their home countries. There they awaited the rise of a new leader to rally them together and infuse them with the will to fight. For the time being, however, the Loyalist campaign in the north had come to a grinding halt.

## Coming Home

Though Sōma Tadashige took part in that last battle under Nitta Yoshisada, he was not among the fifty retainers who had joined Yoshisada on that fateful evening. As an archer he had been quartered in one of the facing strongholds. Had Tadashige and his fellow archers been at Yoshisada's side on that fateful afternoon, events might have taken a different course. As it was, with Yoshisada's death, Tadashige could do little else than unstring his bow and set out on the long journey home. He must have done so with a degree of trepidation, for well over five years had passed since he had set out from Fujigatani castle toward the Ikushina shrine to join his lord in battle and much had happened in the Kantō while he had been away.

At Somoyama castle Tadashige had heard how the Loyalists in the Kantō had fared, and what he had learned had given him great cause for concern. Following Kitabatake Akiie's victorious drive northward, powerful Bakufu forces, under the command of Ishido Yoshifusa, had risen against the Loyalists in the north. Early in 1337, Akiie had been forced to abandon Taga castle and fall back on Ryōzan castle, situated on the crest of the eponymous mountain, some forty miles south of Taga. There he had been joined by reinforcements under the command of Date Yukitomo and Yūki Munehiro, two staunch local Loyalists. Toward the end of 1337 he had felt strong enough to launch another drive toward the capital. On March 29 of the following year, he defeated a Bakufu force at Tennōji in Settsu. But within a week they routed him at the same place. From then on the demoralizing pattern repeated itself, first at Watanabe, then at Abeno. Finally he was hounded down to Sakai, on the Izumi coast, where, broken with fatigue, he died in harness only twenty years old.

## Nenami Okuyama Jion

The former site of Fujigatani castle

The stirring and deeply troubling news had been the last Tadashige's master had learned of the fate of the Loyalists in the east, for shortly afterward, Yoshisada had departed from Somoyama castle to meet his end on the plains of Fukui. Since then, Tadashige had heard no more news from home, but there was little doubt in his mind that the Bakufu had meanwhile reestablished itself in the Kantō.

And sure enough, when the battle-weary Tadashige reached the border of Shimōsa in the summer of 1338, he soon learned that the balance of power in the Kantō had dramatically changed. Following Akiie's death, the Bakufu had quickly begun to reassert its hold over the region. Until then, much of the area surrounding Fujigatani castle had been under the control of Loyalist clans, many of them vassals of the Nittas. Their strongholds were mainly concentrated along the southwestern border of Hitachi province. One of these was Isa castle, on the border with Shimotsuke province. This was the head-

# Famous Samurai: The Two Courts Period

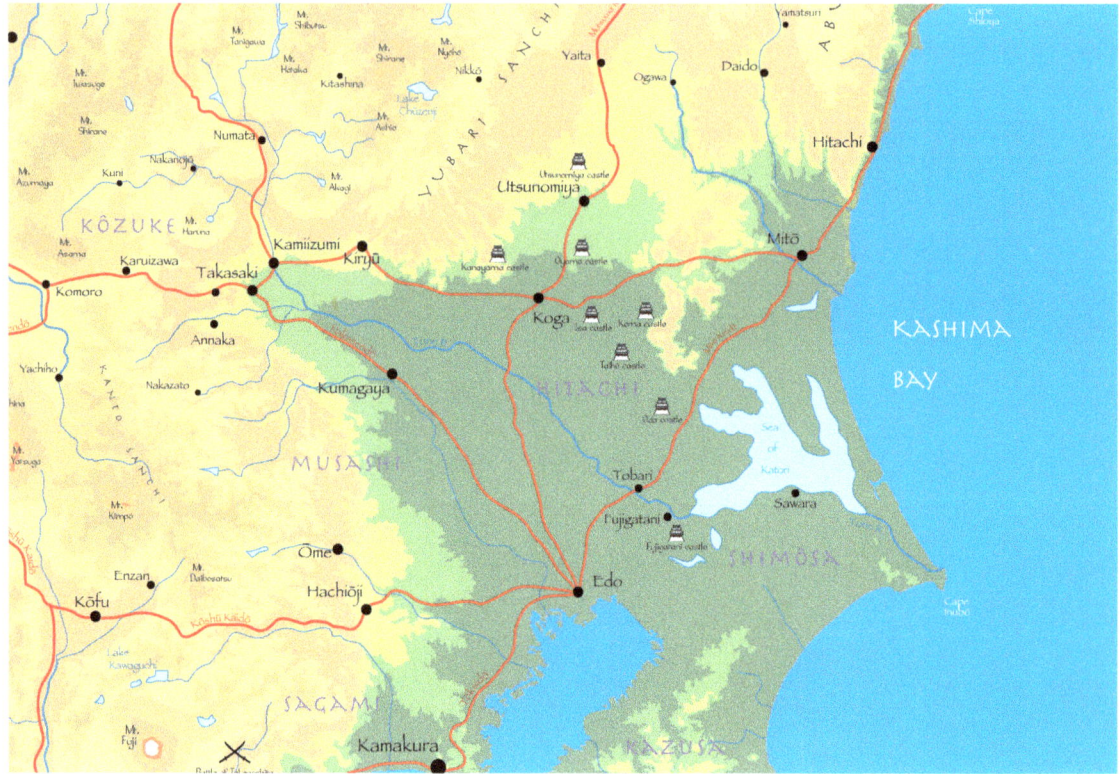

quarters of Date Yukitomo, the warrior who had joined Kitabatake Akiie on his fateful campaign to regain the capital. Somewhat further west, just over the border with Shimotsuke, lay Oyama castle, the stronghold of the Oyama clan. Its previous leader, Oyama Hidetomo, had responded to Yoshisada's call to arms and had died in battle two years later. Another clan member, Oyama Datakaie, had immortalized himself when, in the Battle of Minatogawa, he offered his horse to Yoshisada when the latter's was shot from beneath him, an act for which he had paid with his life. From there, twenty miles northward, lay Utsunomiya castle, the stronghold of the Utsunomiya clan, whose leader, Utsunomiya Kintsuna, had fought alongside the Nitta forces at Takenoshita. Immediately north of Fujigatani, some ten miles into Hitachi, lay Oda castle, the headquarters of the Oda clan, whose leader, Oda Haruhisa, had also fought alongside Akiie's forces two years before. One by one, these Loyalist strongholds were now besieged by Bakufu forces.

The most important among them was perhaps Seki castle. This castle, which was situated in the province of Hitachi, just across the northern border of Shimōsa, was one of the most formidable strongholds in the region. The lord of Seki castle was Seki Munesuke, once one of the more powerful Loyalists in the region but now a besieged man. Already one year prior to Tadashige's return, the Bakufu general Ishido Yoshifusa had laid siege to this bastion of Loyalist resistance. He had been joined by a number of other local Bakufu allies, and one of them was Sōma Chikatane, leader of the Mutsu line of the Sōma clan.

The Mutsu line had sided with the Bakufu forces, and Chikatane had joined Ashikaga Takauji in his drive toward the capital. He had fought with distinction at the Battle of Takenoshita, and later, when they were driven from the capital by Kitabatake Akiie. Following their defeat, he had joined Takauji on his flight to Kyushu and he had been among the forces which had surprised Yoshisada's defenses at the Battle of Minato River. In 1337, he had joined forces with Ishido Yoshifusa to assist the latter in his attempt to regain Bakufu control of the north. They had a hard time in dealing with Kitabatake Akiie, but after Akiie had cleared the field, their hands were free to deal more effectively with the old pockets of Loyalist resistance.

By the time Sōma Tadashige returned from Echizen they had come a long way. Already large tracts of the region had been carved up among the Bakufu allies. Chikatane, too, had reaped his rewards. He had recaptured the family stronghold of Odaka castle and looked to expand his influence southward. In this he was accommodated by a grateful Bakufu, which had granted him control over a large part of the fiefs that formerly belonged to the Shimōsa line of the Sōma clan. Among these possessions was Fujigatani castle, the former property of Tadashige.

And thus, as the fortunes of the Southern Court waned, so did those of the loyal retainer. Having given his all in the course of countless battles over a period of half a decade, Tadashige now met with a fate so many fellow Loyalist retainers were experiencing. Within one and the same year he had lost his master and his estate. Yet even now, after he had lost all that he had been fighting for, Tadashige unswervingly continued to support the Loyalist cause in the Kantō.

## New Hope

That cause gained renewed impetus with the arrival in Hitachi of Kitabatake Chikafusa. Following the death of his son, Akiie, the master tactician had embarked from Ise and arrived on the coast of Hitachi toward the end of October 1338. From there he made his way to Oda castle, from where he conducted the Loyalist campaign against the forces of Ishido Yoshifusa and his Bakufu allies.

Even as he was being besieged by opposing forces, the shrewd and erudite scholar found the time to write one of his celebrated works, *Jinnō shōtōki* (Chronicles of the Direct Descent of Gods and Sovereigns). It was with a specific purpose that he did so, for already prior to his departure from Anou, it had become clear to him that Go-Daigo had not much longer to live. He was to be succeeded by his favorite son, Prince Morinaga. It had been both with the legitimization and the education of the future sovereign in mind that Chikafusa wrote his work. When he completed his work toward the end of 1339, he sent it by sea to the new emperor, for by then word had reached Oda castle that, on September 19 of that same year, Go-Daigo had passed away, clutching in his left hand the scriptures of the Lotus Sutra, and in his right hand a sword, facing northward, toward the capital he had lost. Copies of the *Jinnō shōtōki*, meanwhile, were sent to eastern warlords in an attempt to win them over to the cause of the Southern Court.

Chikafusa's plan was to form a united front with their help and make a drive northward, into Mutsu, and recapture the former Loyalist stronghold of Taga castle. There he hoped to raise yet more troops in order to deal a decisive blow to the Ishido forces, which were now concentrated in the north of Mutsu province. Yet already that plan had been upset when part of the fleet in which he sailed from Izu met with a storm and was forced to return to Izu.

Among those forced to return had been the stout Loyalist Yūki Munehiro. From Ise he had traveled to Anou, where he died after a short illness. Munehiro's death proved to be a double blow to the Loyalists in the north, for his son, Chikatomo, distracted by the loss of his father and intimidated by the growing strength of the Bakufu in the north, remained stubbornly neutral. Yet Chikatomo's cooperation was of crucial importance if Chikafusa's plan was to succeed, for the family stronghold of Shirakawa castle occupied a strategic position. Situated on high ground overlooking the upper waters of the Abukuma River, the stronghold had a commanding sweep over the

Kitabatake Chikafusa, chief strategist behind the Loyalist campaign

# Famous Samurai: The Two Courts Period

A stairway leads up the hill of Shirakawa castle

old road into Mutsu. Of old this place, where the borders of Shimotsuke and Mutsu met, had been the old *seki* or "barrier" by which all movement between the northeastern provinces and the Kantō was controlled. Yet in spite of Chikafusa's efforts, Chikatomo failed to be swayed. As a result, the Loyalist drive northward came to nothing, and the year drew to a close with both parties engaged in what looked like a stalemate.

Then, toward the end of 1339, another large Bakufu force under the command of Kō Morofuyu, the adopted son of Moroyasu, reached the border of Hitachi and began to attack the Loyalist stronghold of Koma castle. Morofuyu failed to take the castle, but well before the year was out he had also reached Oda castle, forcing Chikafusa to decamp to Seki castle. From there Chikafusa had to watch with growing vexation how one by one the Loyalist strongholds fell to the combined onslaught of Morofuyu's and his allies. Pinned down in Seki castle, Chikafusa now placed his hopes on his second son, Akinobu, whom he had earlier dispatched northward in an effort to raise troops among the Loyalists in Mutsu. By the summer of 1340 Akinobu had installed himself in Hiyoriyama castle, in the northern highlands of Mutsu. From there he hoped to march on Taga castle, some twenty miles southeast along the coast. It took until the autumn of 1341 before Akinobu was ready to do battle with Ishido's troops. Both forces converged on the Sendai Plains. There in the basin of the San no Hasama River, they entrenched themselves behind makeshift defenses and embarked on a battle of attrition that lasted throughout the winter. Even when spring came the stalemate continued, as many soldiers, sick of the continuous fighting amid the freezing cold, had deserted their colors over the previous months, so that those who remained behind made little headway.

By the summer of 1342 most of the Loyalist strongholds down in Hitachi had fallen. Only two fortresses, that of Taihō and Seki castle, situated on either side of the Taihō Lagoon, were still holding out.

# Famous Samurai: The Two Courts Period

Taihō castle, situated on the southern end of the marshes, was the stronghold of the Shimotsuma clan, which descended from the Oyama. Their leader, Shimotsuma Masayasu, had fought off Morofuyu's forces with success for the better part of two years. It was their very position, at both ends of the marshes, that gave the castles their united strength, as communications, troops, and provisions could be freely ferried from one castle to the other as required, without any interference of the besieging forces. Seki castle in particular benefited from the natural protection offered by the marshes. It stood on a narrow peninsula that projected southward into the marshes, thus creating a natural moat. The only access over land was from the north and it was this side of the castle that was most strongly defended. Changing his strategy, Morofuyu now set out to literally undermine the Loyalist defenses by digging a tunnel, right up to the castle's main tower. Yet before his men

Yoshino the seat of the Southern Court

had reached their objective, those within the castle had caught wind of what was going on. Unable to venture outside the castle's defenses, they began to dig their own tunnel, undermining that of the enemy and causing it to collapse. A large number of Morofuyu's men were buried alive and all digging activities were ceased. Morofuyu now tried his luck over water and had his men build large boats, but here too he was far from successful.

In this fashion the siege of the two castles dragged on for another year. Already it had become one of the longest drawn out sieges in Japan's history of siege warfare. Both castles had held out for the better part of three years, and those within were suffering the effects of malnutrition and unrelenting hostilities. Yet somehow their spirits remained undaunted, inspired as they were by the leadership of Chikafusa, the embodiment of the Loyalist cause.

That seemingly indomitable spirit received a final and crushing blow in the summer of 1343, when word reached Seki castle that, in spite of Chikafusa's efforts, Yūki Chikatomo had joined the Bakufu. Takauji had won him over with promises of land and rank. With Chikatomo's defection, the door to the north had effectively been closed and with it any prospects of a successful drive northward or even a union with Akinobu's forces was irretrievably scuttled. For another few months Seki castle held out, defended by only a few hundred desperate men. Finally, on November 11, at the end of a dreadful and demoralizing year, the castle fell. Its master, Seki Munesuke, committed suicide. So did Shimotsuma Masayasu, whose castle fell only one day later. With the loss of both strongholds the last hopes of a Loyalist revival in the north evaporated. Chikafusa managed to escape. He fled back over sea to Ise, and from thence to Anou and the safety of the Yoshino Mountains, from where he continued to lead the campaign of the Southern Court.

For the few scattered remains of the Loyalist cause in the Kantō, a bleak and demoralizing period now began. So, too, for Sōma Tadashige. He had fought under the two leading lights of the Loyalist campaign, yet he was not to reap the rewards of his unstinting efforts. For him the glory days of fighting under Nitta Yoshisada were gone. Never again would he be on the side of victorious forces, and never again would he be the master of his own fiefdom. Instead, he was to spend his last days as a *rōnin*, a masterless samurai, who depended on the hospitality of townsmen and peasants for a roof over his head.

# Famous Samurai: The Two Courts Period

## Adopted

*The hamlet of Imajuku along the Nakasendō*

It was during these uncertain years, when the fate of the Southern Court hung in the balance, that Sōma Yoshimoto and his brother Tanemochi were born. It is not clear where the two brothers first saw the light of day, but they must have had an unsettled childhood, drifting from place to place as their father sought to escape the clutches of a Bakufu that was gaining ever more influence over the Kantō. It was a hard and hardening existence, with little room for the innocent play of childhood. And though the two brothers must have sensed the threat to which they were exposed, at least they lived in the comfort of their father's protection.

That protection fell away in 1356, when Sōma Tadashige was killed. It was not on the battlefield that the brave warrior found his end. Sadly the records do not reveal the identity of the murderer, yet it is quite certain that

# Nenami Okuyama Jion

it was one of Sōma Chikatane's henchmen. It was Chikatane, after all, who had unrightfully seized Tadashige's estate of Fujigatani in 1338. What is certain is that Tadashige's death was not redressed, for both his sons had to flee their current abode to escape their father's plight. Being the oldest of the two, and thus his father's heir by right, Yoshimoto's life was most at risk and with no adoptive father at hand his only chance of survival was to go into hiding. Under cover of the night the young boy was spirited away by his wet nurse. She took him southward, across the border with the province of Musashi, to Imajuku, a hamlet along the Nakasendō, where they remained in hiding for the next two years. Then, in 1358, at the age of seven, the fugitive was entrusted to the care of an itinerant monk from the Jōdo sect. The monk took the young boy to his home town of Fujisawa, on the Bay of Sagami. There the young boy was interned in the Yugyō monastery, and given the Buddhist name by which he came to be known, Nenami.

Fujisawa, with in the background, atop the hill, the Yuguō temple

# Famous Samurai: The Two Courts Period

For the next few years Nenami led the life of any young apprentice monk, rising early for a day of hard menial labor, scriptural study, and long sessions of spiritual meditation. Yet despite the profound change that had taken place in his life, it seems that Nenami warmed to monastery life, for the young boy soon learned to adopt to the harsh and disciplining dictates of his new environment and applied himself to his studies. Given Nenami's choices in later life these years of seclusion were of seminal influence.

While Nenami found solace in the distractions of a totally new and spiritual existence, his life as a monk continued to be overshadowed by a dark and at times unbearable truth. Three thing weighed on his mind: he was of noble birth, he was his father's rightful heir, and his father had been treacherously killed. Despite the outward guise of spiritual serenity, deep within, the young lay monk was consumed by a deep and burning hatred of those who had marred his father's name and had forced him to conceal his own, and much of the ardor with which he applied himself to his studies was fueled by the very same fire that had been kindled by his father's death. Yet even within the quietude of the Yugyō monastery there were ways for the angry young youth to channel his anger.

Compared to the Ikkō, Tendai, and Nichiren's belligerent Hokke sect, the Jōdo sect to which Nenami's monastery belonged was a relatively peaceful one. But even at the Yugyō monastery there were many opportunities for an apprentice monk to hone his skills in the martial arts. It is clear that already at this early age, Nenami was intent on revenging his father. This is revealed simply by his choice of weapon. The natural choice for Nenami would have been the longbow. Archery was the art of the elite and the nobility. It had been the art in which his father had excelled and Nenami must have had fond memories of how, as a small boy, he was instructed in this noble art by his father. In such a choice he could have easily been accommodated, as archery was, and still is, practiced by monks in many a temple. Nor did he choose the *naginata* or *yari*, the standard repertoire of the warrior monks. Instead he chose the sword, the undisputed weapon for man-to-man combat and the weapon of choice for those who engaged in duels.

In his choice of weapon, then, the apprentice monk faced a major obstacle. Even among the warrior monks few were truly adept in the art of

# Nenami Okuyama Jion

Monasteries during Japan's middle ages were far more than mere religious centers, they were centers not only of political, but even military power. Many of the thousands of monasteries that adorned the Japanese landscape came closer to fortified strongholds than places of pious meditation. They had complex defenses, manned by garrisons of *sōhei*, the notorious and battle-hardened warrior monks. This was usually done in groups of several hundred, although their ranks could easily be multiplied by the ring of an alarm bell. Within the temple grounds young monks would practice the art of combat from early dawn till late at night. Such practice was no mere pastime but a tradition born out of necessity and pursued with a spiritual devotion that had its equal only in the warrior's pride in ancestry.

The preferred weapon of the warrior monks was the *yari* (the Japanese javelin) or the *naginata* (the pole sword), weapons of up to several yards in length, with which one could keep even a mounted opponent at bay. So well organized were the main Buddhist sects of Nenami's day, that temple complexes such as that of the Enryaku and the Heisen were considered impregnable. If they did not already feel constrained by religious inhibitions most of Japan's medieval warlords prudently chose to form alliances with, rather than antagonize the more powerful Buddhist sects. It was to take right up until the end of the fifteenth century, when Oda Nobunaga, the first of Japan's three great unifiers, set out to destroy these bulwarks of religious resistance before the power of the sects was finally and irrevocably broken.

*Sōhei*, recognizable by their typical white headgear, gathered on the porch of the Mii temple in Ōmi

# Famous Samurai: The Two Courts Period

Archer monks at practice

swordsmanship, and in the seclusion of the Yugyō monastery there was little opportunity for an apprentice to hone his skills in the art of fencing. For three years Nenami persevered in his practice, relying largely on his instincts and learning what basic skills he could from those who had some knowledge of the art. Given his objective, it was a highly unsatisfactory way of going about things, and already a few years after he had entered holy orders, the young boy reached a point where he felt he was not making enough progress. Too young yet to leave the protection of the monastery, but too advanced to stay, the only logical choice for Nenami to advance his budding martial skills was to move to a monastery where he stood a better chance to be exposed to those who had mastered the art he pursued. And thus, at the tender age of ten, Nenami set out along the Tōkaidō and traveled down to Kyoto, carrying a letter of recommendation for the abbot of the Anba temple.

# To Kyoto

To any monk intent on pursuing the peaceful path of spiritual enlightenment, setting out for the capital at the time in which Nenami did would have run counter to their deepest convictions. But for a young man eager to acquire the highest level of martial attainment it was an understandable, albeit daring move. Following the first hostilities in the aftermath of the Kenmu Restoration the geographical dispersion of the two rival factions had soon caused the conflict to spread to other regions of Japan. Yet throughout the long period of conflict that followed, the capital and the surrounding home provinces remained the most fiercely contested. The capital, after all, was the place where the emperor had held court since the ninth century. It was the jewel in the crown—a magic wand that gave almost instant legitimacy to the actions of those who possessed it, as well as immense powers of influence. And thus, while many a battle was fought elsewhere throughout the following decades, the capital was to remain the center stage on which the two factions fought out their most poignant battles for supremacy. It was this aspect of the conflict between the Southern and Northern Courts, combined with the deep involvement of Japan's major religious sects in that self same conflict that made Nenami's choice such a logical one. For it was here, at Japan's political center of gravity, that the intensity of battle caused many of the methods and means of combat to spill over into the temple grounds.

The struggle for Kyoto reached its climax between 1352 and 1355. During this period the fortunes of both Courts changed with almost every month. No sooner had one army driven out the other to lay claim of the city as its own, or it was forced to make a tactical withdrawal into one of the surrounding provinces. At times it took months for the defeated army to regroup and recapture the capital, at other times it was only a matter of days. Neither party, however, managed to hold the city for longer than a year. Nor did any of the two parties make any effort to spare their coveted trophy, so that by the end of this period of mayhem nearly all the royal palaces, the mansions of the nobility, and offices of the ministers of state had been destroyed. Large tracts of the city lay utterly bare. All that remained of the capital's former splendor were ruins overgrown with grass and piles of bleached bones of the dead.

In the years after 1355 the capital remained under the control of the Northern Court. Not that its citizens could now go about their business in peace. The constant quarreling among high ranking generals ensured that the great number of Bakufu troops stationed in the capital were more pre-

## Famous Samurai: The Two Courts Period

occupied with factional fighting than maintaining order, so that even in the few uncertain interludes of relative peace, when its streets were not the scene of full-blown warfare, peace came closer to a state of subdued anarchy. So preoccupied were those who led the Bakufu that many of its leading lights turned their backs on the Bakufu and went over to the side of the Southern Court. Partly as a result of these defections the position of the Loyalist forces was much improved by the time Nenami arrived in Kyoto, And it was early in 1362, only months after the young Buddhist monk had taken up lodgings in the Anba temple on the city's outskirts, that the Loyalists launched yet another campaign to take the capital.

The Two Courts period was not the first time the capital had been the stage of warfare. During twelfth century the capital had already seen hard fighting, first during the Hōgen Rebellion of 1156, and the during the Heiji Rebellion of 1160. In both cases, however, much of the fighting centered around the imperial palace. During the five year Genpei war (1180–85), which claimed the lives of some twenty thousand , the capital again was spared, as this rivalry between the Taira and Minamoto clans encompassed much of the realm and fought out largely outside the capital (though a number of building, including the Taira headquarters of Rokuhara and the Emperor's quarters of the Hōjūjidono went up in flames).

## Nenami Okuyama Jion

As the word spread that the Loyalist were advancing, and the Bakufu troops began to barricade the capital's seven entrances, the main roads converging on the capital once again grew dense with people. On their way out were women, children, and the elderly, whole families carrying what little possessions they had in the hope of finding safety with relatives in the countryside. On their way in were bowyers, smiths and harnessers carrying their merchandise and tools of trade to set up shop within the protection of the temple grounds to make their living on the deaths of others. Among the many mercenaries that converged upon the capital were the timeless soldiers of fortune, following the noxious trail of death and destruction and selling

Much of the ancient capital, therefore, was still in tact on the outbreak of war between the Northern and Southern Courts. Yet even during this war, which did at times center around the capital as the seat of the Northern (Bakufu) Court, much of the capital was spared as troop movements were fast with volatile battle fronts, while all of the major battles (notably at Sunomatogawa, Ichi no Dani, and Dan no Ura were fought in other parts of the country.

It was only later, during the prolonged and terrible trench warfare of the Ōnin War (1467–77), which saw the outbreak of the Warring States Period, that large swathes of the capital were reduced to ashes and that much of its splendor was lost forever.

## Famous Samurai: The Two Courts Period

their deadly skills to whoever paid most. It was not uncommon, even for monasteries—especially those who did not have at their disposal the garrisons of *sōhei* commanded by the powerful Ikkō and Tendai sects—to offer the mercenaries food and shelter in exchange for protection. And it was one such mercenary, a man of Chinese origin whose name has not been recorded for posterity, who took up lodgings in the Anba temple shortly after Nenami, and who first introduced the young monk to the ancient secrets of Chinese swordsmanship.

The Loyalist campaign of 1362 failed in its objective and once again the capital was brought under Bakufu control. For the young monk it must have been a time at once moving and yet deeply upsetting. He had seen the Loyalist troops in action—forces that were fighting for the same cause for which his father had fought, and for a brief but exhilarating moment he, like his father, felt that its goal was an attainable one. Their presence, however brief

Kyoto's Anba temple in Nenami's day

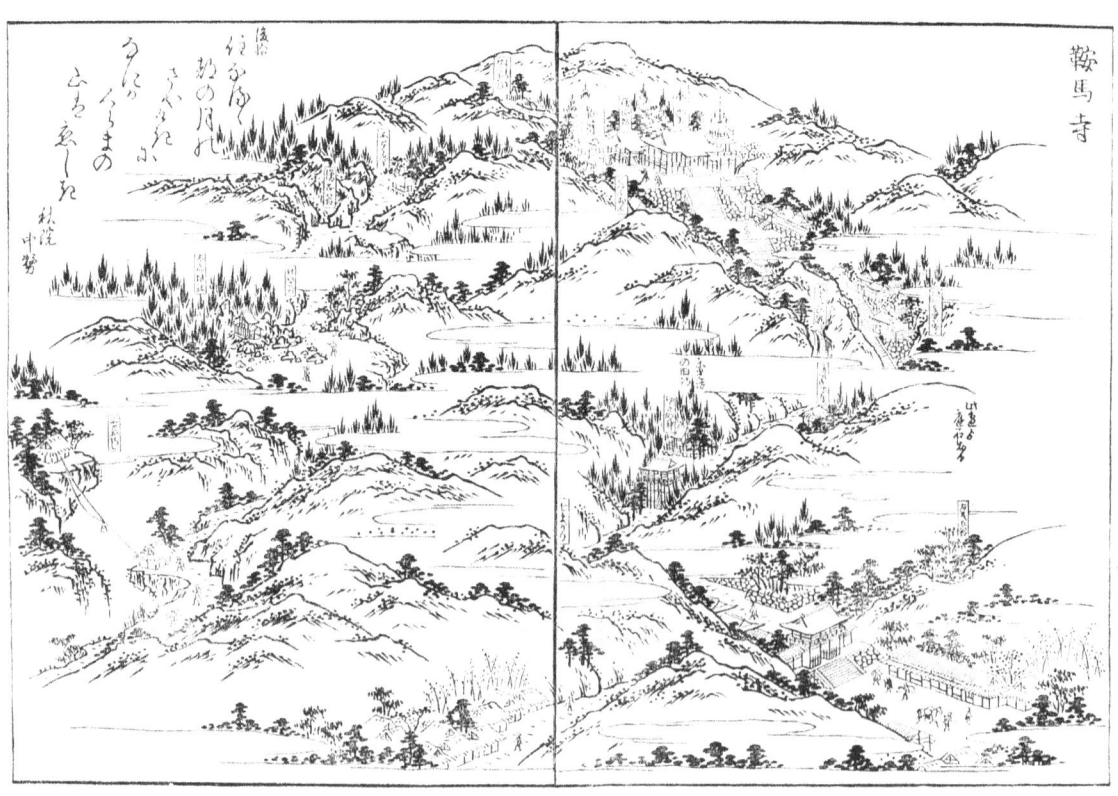

# Nenami Okuyama Jion

The Anba temple today

it may have been, deepened his sense of destiny and lent particular immediacy to his martial studies. For the Chinese mercenary, by contrast, the following years must have been years of relative ease, for it is unlikely that he saw much action. The assault of 1362 was the last serious attempt of the Loyalists to win the capital. As many as four times they had marched on the capital. Each time they had managed to evict the Bakufu forces, but each time, too, they had been forced to retreat, the fourth time after no more than three weeks. In the course of these vast and costly campaigns the Loyalists had utterly spent themselves. Unable to maintain the momentum in the Home Provinces, they were forced to follow Takauji's example. They retreated to Kyushu, where, like Takauji, they set up their headquarters in the

# Famous Samurai: The Two Courts Period

The inner grounds of the Anba temple

Dazaifu, the former government offices on the island. The change in the Loyalist fortunes was also to affect the immediate future of the young monk, for early in 1366, without any prospect of work, the Chinese mercenary left the Anba temple to seek his fortunes elsewhere.

Without an instructor Nenami, too, decided to pick up his few belongings and take to the road, not, however, to Shimōsa, but toward Kamakura. He was still only sixteen years old, and though by now an accomplished swordsman, it had chiefly been the Chinese art of combat he had thus far practiced. In view of his objective he must have been keen also to familiarize himself with a more indigenous style of fencing, if only to widen the range of his techniques. And thus, early 1366, the young swordsman-monk arrived in Kamakura to take up residence in the Jufuku temple and pursue his studies under the tutelage of Shinsō Eisuke, one of the few Zen monks of his time versed in the tenets of Japanese swordsmanship.

## To Kyushu

Early in 1368, word reached the Jufuku temple that the Bakufu had launched a major campaign to crush what remained of the Loyalist forces who had entrenched themselves in Japan's most southern island of Kyushu. That campaign, too, failed in its objective—it even failed to cross the Straits of Shimonoseki—but it was clear that the outlook of the Southern Court was bleaker than ever. In spite of the attempt on Kyoto of 1362, the fortunes of the Southern Court had been dwindling ever since it had lost its great strategist, Kitabatake Chikafusa. He had died in 1358 following a short illness. After that, the only two things that gave the Loyalists hope were the internal feuds among Bakufu generals in Kyoto and their new leader, Prince Kaneyoshi, one of Go-Daigo's few surviving sons. Under Kaneyoshi's leadership the remaining Loyalist forces had managed to consolidate their power base by bringing most of Kyushu under their control.

Stirred into action by these new developments, the now eighteen-year-old monk set out from Kamakura in the autumn of 1368 and traveled southward. Embarking from Sakai, he crossed the Inland Sea, to finally make land on the southern island of Kyushu. There he entered holy orders at the Dazaifu Tenmangu, a sprawling temple complex built on the southern slopes of Mount Hōman in honor of the great Sugawara Michizane.

## A Last Stand

Though Nenami was a young man with deep intellectual interests, it had not been out of reverence for Michizane's memory that he had chosen the Dazaifu Tenmangu as his new abode. Indeed, the very choice of temple was a direct indication where Nenami's loyalties lay, for it so happened that the temple was built on the former grounds of the Dazaifu. Established in 701, the Dazaifu had functioned as the local governmental office charged with military defenses and diplomatic relations with the mainland during the Heian Period. Since the establishment of the Kamakura Bakufu (1185–1333), the office had gone into decline, functioning in name only. With the arrival of prince Kaneyoshi, it had found a new purpose, for he had used it as the headquarters from which to bring Kyushu under his control. Now he chose it as the place from which he was to make his last stand.

Partly as a result of the Bakufu's own tardiness, it took Kaneyoshi little effort to frustrate the 1368 campaign. Things changed, however, when, in 1370, the Bakufu appointed Imagawa Sadayo as *Kyushu tandai* or High Commissioner for Kyushu. Sadayo was not the average run-of-the-mill warrior.

Already in Nenami's day, the Dazaifu Tenmangu boasted a long history that went all the way back to the beginning of the tenth century.

From its very founding the temple had been closely associated with Sugawara Michizane. Michizane had been one of the great scholars and administrators of the Heian period (794–1189), the golden age of the Japanese imperial court. He had lived during the second half of the ninth century and had risen to high rank by the end of the century, but in 901 his brilliant career had come to an ignominious end when he was accused of plotting against the throne and exiled to Kyushu. Forced to leave his wife behind in the capital, the fifty-six-year-old Michizane had made the long journey south, well aware that his days in the sun were numbered. His only consolation was the company of his son and daughter, but not long after he had taken up his new and insignificant post as local administrator his son died. The sensitive courtier never recovered from the blow. His health failed, and in 903 he died a broken man.

Soon the diviners of his time found reasons to believe that the great scholar had not found peace in death, for in the years that followed, the capital was struck by an inexplicable chain of calamities.

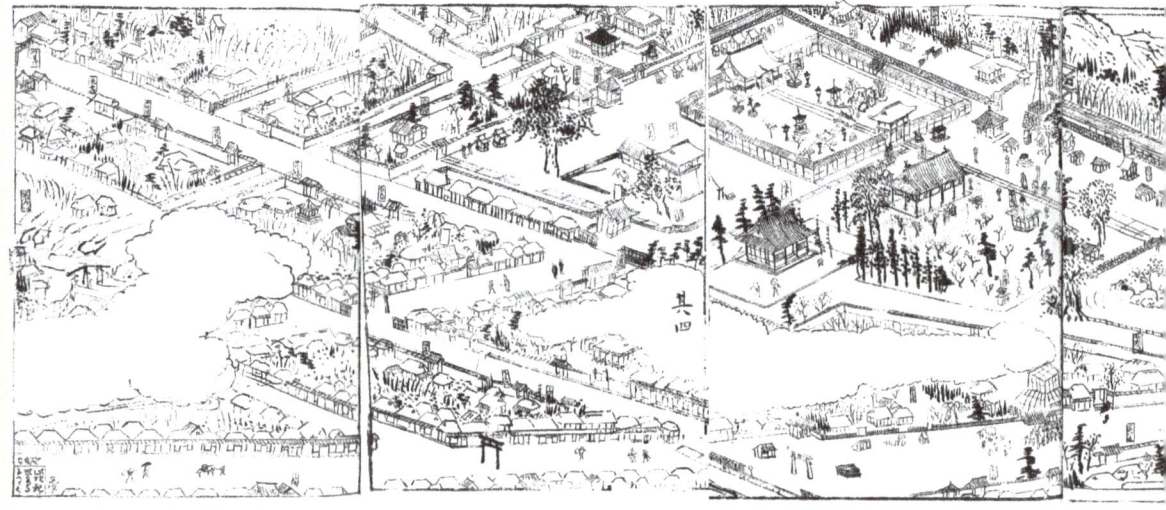

*Nenami Okuyama Jion*

A scion of a house of great repute, the general was a man of noble birth, whose father, Imagawa Norikuni, had spent most of his life campaigning for Ashikaga Takauji. Sadayo, too, had made a name for himself, not only by his military feats, but also by his exquisite poetry. He was a reflective and deeply spiritual man, who had just taken the tonsure under the name of Ryōshun when he was summoned to Kyoto to receive his brief.

The first omens of Michizane's wrath manifested themselves when, one by one, the men who had conspired in his downfall died under mysterious circumstances. In the hope to appease Michizane's spirit, in 923 the then emperor, Daigo, posthumously reinstated the former minister, but the series of calamities failed to cease. In 930, the Great Audience Hall of the palace was hit by lightning. It caught fire and a number of courtiers perished in the flames, including the man who claimed to have overheard Michizane's admission of guilt. For weeks on end ferocious rainstorms continued to torment the capital until, at long last, racked by the strain of fear and guilt, the emperor himself died at the age of forty-five. After that the calamities seemed to have ceased, but the reverence paid to Michizane continued.

In 905 an altar was established near his grave site, and it was at the same place that, in 919 the foundations were laid for the Dazaifu Tenmangu. The temple was to become a place of worship for the spirit of that great and gifted scholar, who, in time, became deified as the Tenman Daijizai Tenjin, the Heaven-filling Supreme Lord and Heavenly Diety, the god of learning and calligraphy

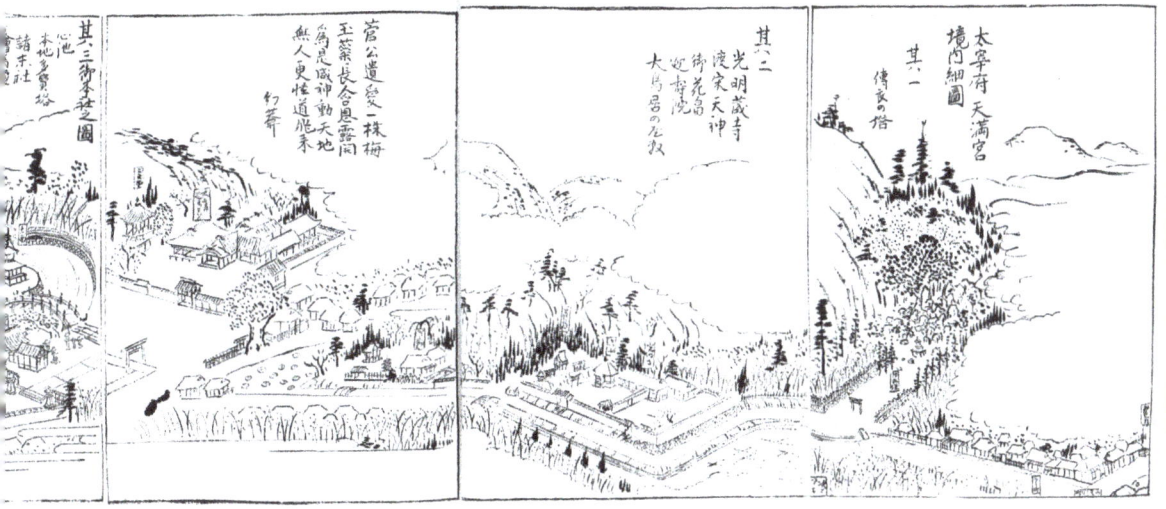

# Famous Samurai: The Two Courts Period

Sadayo proved to be the right man at the right moment. He left Kyoto early in 1370 and proceeded southward at a leisurely pace. In the summer of 1371 his son, Yoshinori, departed with a large force from Onomichi, only a few miles from where Takauji and his brother had landed on their return from Kyushu, and sailed for the Bay of Beppu, in the eastern province of Bungo. There he besieged and captured Takasaki castle and stubbornly resisted belated attempts by the Loyalists to evict him. Not much later, another Imagawa clan member, this time Sadayo's younger brother, Tadaaki, landed in the province of Hizen, on the western side of Kyushu. At first he ran into stiff opposition, but by the end of the year he was able to reach Matsuura, some fifty miles westward along the coast from the Dazaifu. Then, early in 1372, seeing that all conditions for a successful move had been met, Sadayo himself departed from Shimonoseki with a large force and landed at Kokura, on the northern tip of the island. From there he began to march southward,

The main hall of the Dazaifu Tenmangu

62

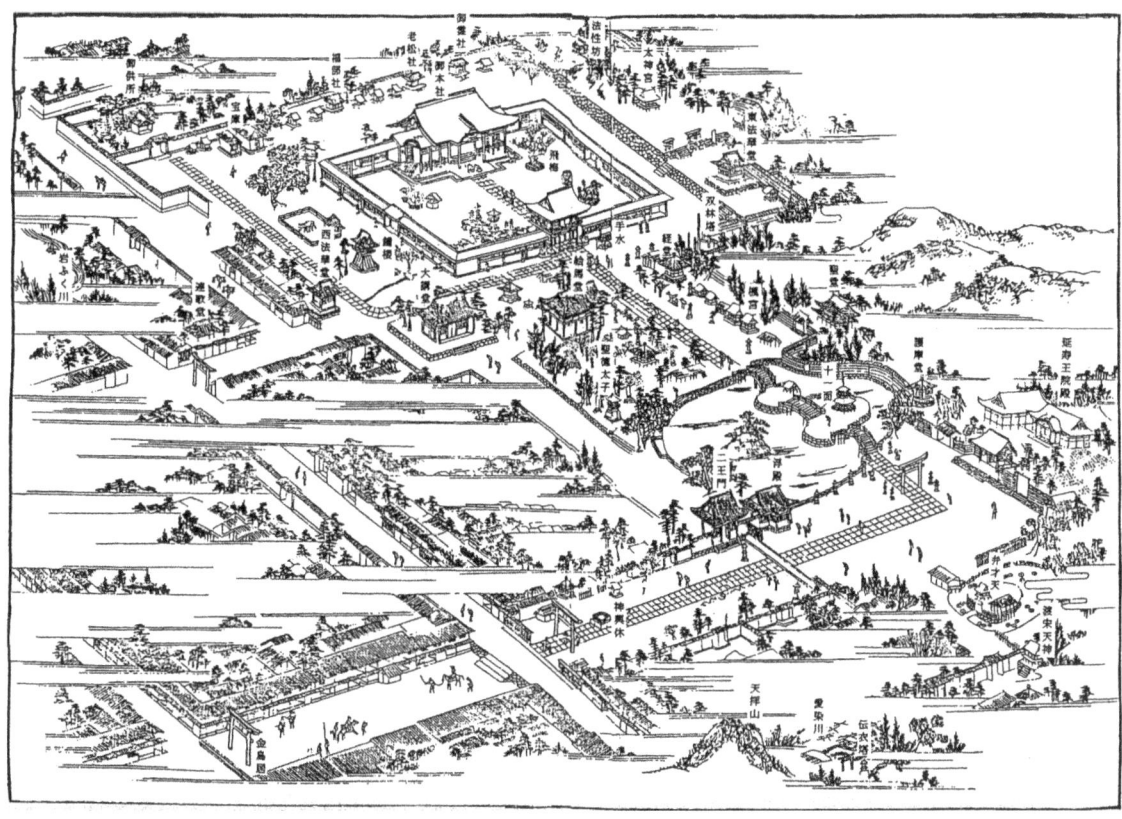

Close-up map of the Dazaifu Tenmangu

straight toward the Dazaifu. So did the two forces under the command of his brother and his son, Yoshinori from the west, Tadaaki from the south. The three forces converged on the Daizaifu that same summer.

It is almost certain that Nenami actively took part in the battles that were fought practically outside the gate of the Dazaifu Tenmangu. Not only would it have been a welcome opportunity to hone his fencing skills in the heat of battle, but it was also a chance to fight for the same cause to which his father had dedicated his life, and thus satisfy his deeply ingrained feelings of filial piety. As it was, that cause was a lost one. Toward the end of September 1372, after only a few months of resistance, the Dazaifu fell into the hands of the Bakufu. Prince Kaneyoshi fled to the safety of Mount Kōra, in the province of Chikugo, from where he continued to resist the Bakufu forces.

It had taken Prince Kaneyoshi twelve long years of hard work to subdue

# Famous Samurai: The Two Courts Period

Kyushu. Making good use of the historical function of the Dazaifu, he had even managed to establish diplomatic relations with Ming China, thus further enhancing the prestige of the Southern Court, both abroad and at home. All this had been lost almost overnight. It was not yet the end of the Loyalist cause. Many more battles were to follow, but from this point onward the contest for supremacy itself had been settled irrevocably in favor of the Bakufu. For two more decades the two courts were to face each other across numerous battlefields throughout Kyushu. Then, late in 1392, the Southern Court responded to an overture by Takauji's grandson, Ashikaga Yoshimitsu. In December of that year, some fifty years after Emperor Go-Daigo had caused a rift in the imperial house by fleeing into the Yoshino mountains, the fighting parties came to a settlement. The two courts were to be unified and the succession was to alternate between the two imperial lines.

# Revenge

Long before the last warrior in the contest between the two courts had fallen, Nenami had quit the scene. It is not clear from the records when the now grown man had finally come to address the burning question that had come to dominate his life. It was probably some years after the fall of the Dazaifu, during one of the many battles that followed, that that inescapable moment finally came. He was now in his twenties, in the prime of his life and, given his upbringing and character, must have felt all-consuming and overpowering urge to revenge his father and thus unburden himself. It is not hard to imagine how, fighting for the very same cause as his father, in the very heat of some pitched battle on some forsaken battlefield, the young swordsman reached a point where he felt confident of his mastery of the sword. It must have been at that point that his most haunting question was finally and affirmatively answered: was he worth his mettle and was he was up to the task of confronting the man who had slain his father? It had been the pursuit of that question that had caused the young boy to set out on the long and meandering road with such unwavering determination a decade before, and it was the need to answer that question that now drove the grown man to shed his Buddhist robes, assume his original name of Sōma Yoshimoto, and set sail from Kyushu to travel all the way back to his place of birth. There he sought out the man who had robbed him of his childhood, and took his head, thereby fulfilling his filial obligation to his father.

It was undoubtedly to protect Nenami's relatives and descendants that the family records remain silent about the identity of the man or men who finally felt the young man's wrath. Probably, it was one of Sōma Chikatane's henchmen who had been sent out to dispatch the rightful claimant to the Fuijigatani estate. Yet there is another, more tantalizing possibility, a scenario that made it all the more important to observe such discretion, and that scenario is that the man on whom Nenami wreaked his revenge was none other than Chikatane himself. Chikatane, after all, would have been the man who had given the order to eliminate the rightful heir. As such, he bore the moral responsibility for the death of Tadashige. Indeed, even as the recipient of the Fujigatani estate he could be considered culpable. To the young orphan that culpability must have been made all the more unpalatable by the total impunity with which it was committed. Nor would Nenami have been able to find any refuge in poetic justice, for, in the end, the Bakufu forces were victorious, and, unlike most of the warriors of his age, Chikatane survived the many battles in which he had taken part, living on to enjoy great prestige and fortune. Already in 1338 he had been appointed Military Commissioner for the coastal roads connecting a number of districts in Mutsu. Over the years he gradually climbed in rank until, in 1351, he was appointed Military Commissioner for Mutsu and Hitachi. Then, in 1358, he transferred the family estate to his son Tanetomo and retired into religion under the spiritual name of Seishin. After that, nothing more is heard of Chikatane, and it is here where the conditions are met for that other scenario, for it is not wholly impossible that in his spiritual retreat, as he contemplated on his previous life as a warrior and the many wrongs committed, his past finally caught up with him through the sword of the young Yoshimoto.

Though Nenami had restored honor to his father's name, and thereby to his own line of the Sōma clan, there was no estate to which he could return. It had been fifteen years since his father had been assassinated. Since then the Fujigatani estate had been confiscated by the Mutsu line of the Sōma clan. In a world in which land was won and lost simply on the strength of allegiance, there was no room for legal disputes over succession rights. By now most of the provinces in the north were firmly under Bakufu control and given that both Nenami and his father had fought on the side of the Loyalists, it was a simple fact of life that they had lost what had once rightfully been theirs. It is even questionable whether, had he been able to do so, Nenami would have wanted to step in his father's footsteps. For while he was of aristocratic birth, he had spent most of his life in the confines of monasteries and he had no training nor any experience in the leading of men, let alone how to manage an estate.

The young warrior had reached another crossroads in a life dedicated to one goal only: to redress the wrong that had been done to his father. Now that wrong had been redressed, and it seemed that much of what he had learned—the techniques of the Chinese mercenary at the Anba temple, the Japanese techniques of Shinsō Eisuke at the Jufuku temple—had lost their meaning. At the same time, his Buddhist learning and his unparalleled mastery of the sword were the only assets in life he had. Through a quirk of fate, these two so disparate attainments had become the two things that defined his existence. He was still young, with much of his life before him, and if he were to give any purpose to his remaining years he had better build on what he had. And thus the young man who had been born a potential warlord relinquished his rightful claims and, assuming the Buddhist name of Jion, set out on a life of so-called *musha shugyō*, or knight-errantry.

Though uncommon for a monk, Jion's choice was not unique. Indeed, many a young swordsman in Jion's day chose this form of errantry. For the young monk there was even a familiar aspect in his newly chosen life. The practice of *musha shugyō* went all the way back to the ancient practices of the *yamabushi*, the enigmatic mountain monks of the inhospitable Japanese Alps,

Old map of the Sōma fiefs in Shimōsa

those who chose this type of errantry committed themselves to an austere life of celibacy and self-denial. In this, it very much resembled the aesthetic practice of the monastery, the so-called *shugyō*, the aim of which was to deepen one's spiritual awareness through self-reflection and study and root out any worldly weaknesses. While the true aim of *musha shugyō* was to conquer the enemy within, hardened warriors often used the opportunities of a life on the road to test their prowess in duels with proponents of another school of fencing. The outcome of these so-called *taryū shiai* were often deadly. If not, the defeated party might chose to submit themselves to their superiors and, if accepted, follow them on their travels around the country in the hope of ultimately emulating and perhaps surpassing their teachers. It was not uncommon, then, to encounter on the road between one village and another, a master swordsmen followed by a group of acolytes. In view of his monastic background, Jion, too, was to attract his share of disciples in the course of his travels, but in general he seemed to have shied away from *taryū shiai* or any other forms of ostentation.

Little is known about Jion's life on the road, for shortly after his return to Shimōsa the trail of his life runs cold. A more immediate reason for his urge to stay out of the public eye is undoubtedly the score he had only recently settled. That such an urge existed is further borne out by his adoption of yet another spiritual name, even though he had already received one on his entry into the Yugyō monastery, some fifteen years earlier. If, moreover, he was the man responsible for Chikatane's untimely end, such a flight into obscurity would have been a bare necessity, as there would have been only few places in a Bakufu controlled country that offered refuge to a man responsible for the assassination of one of its Military Commissioners. The fact remains that hardly anything can be said with any certainty about Jion actions and whereabouts for the next few decades.

# Setting Down

It is more than twenty years later, at the turn of the fourteenth century, that Jion's name resurfaces in the historical records when, having reached the age

## Nenami Okuyama Jion

A *musha shugyōsha* is about to draw his sword. Note the top of his sword's hilt. Based on the itinerant monk's staff, or *shakujō*, it has an ornate brass extension from which several rings hang freely.

Though the *shakujō* itself could also be wielded as a weapon to ward of wild animals, here its top has been adopted to denote the spiritual nature of the warrior's journey.

The jingling rings are there to chase away insects and other small animals (sentient beings in Buddhist lore) from the carrier's path and save them from being accidentally trodden on. The rings also serve to alert those within earshot that a *shugyōsha* is approaching, thus warning those who might have evil intentions.

Four rings represent the Four Noble Truths, six rings (as depicted here) the Six Perfections, and twelve rings represent the Twelvefold Chain of Cause and Effect.

# Famous Samurai: The Two Courts Period

*Musha shugyōsha* face each other off in a *taryū shiai*

of fifty-eight, and weary of a life on the road, he finally decided to settle down. Unable to return to his home province of Shimōsa, the old monk, now known by the name of Jion, chose to spend the remaining days of his life in the village of Namiai, in the province of Shinano.

It is not clear what led Jion to this particular place, in an environment so unlike the one in which he grew up. It may well have been his affinity with the *yamabushi* that drew him to this part of Japan, for the village of Namiai lay at the very heart of *yamabushi* country, safely tucked away between the towering mountains of the Japanese Alps. For it was here, along the Wachino River that, in the summer of 1408, Jion conducted the consecration rites of a temple he gave the name Chōfukuji, the temple of lasting bliss.

To mark his return to a sedentary monastic life, and perhaps to ensure his continued safety, Jion once more assumed a new name, this time calling himself Nendai Oshō. To the swordsmen of his day, however, he was best known as Nenami Jion, for though he had again entered holy orders, and in spite of his considerable age, Jion continued both to teach and to practice his particular style of swordsmanship. He gave his style of fencing the name of Nen-ryū, the "sense" or "thought" school of swordsmanship, taken from the first character of the name he had been given some fifty years before,

## Nenami Okuyama Jion

when he had first taken the tonsure at the Yugyō monastery in Fujisawa. He had visited the remotest corners of Japan and had met with people of all walks of life. In all those travels and encounters his constant endeavor had been to learn and to widen his mental horizons. He had deepened his spiritual understanding by seeking out and learning from *tatsujin*, those who had reached a higher level of attainment, whether in the realm of Buddhist religion or in the field of martial arts. Now, in his old age, he himself had become a *tatsujin*—a bearing point for other to steer by. Almost as a matter of course, then, the Chōfuku temple became a place of pilgrimage, visited by swordsmen from all over the country, young and old alike, who had set out on their own *musha shugyō* in the hope of attaining martial enlightenment.

It is hardly surprising, then, that in the course of his life Jion gathered around him a large group of followers. Only a small number among them were to be initiated into the deepest secrets, the mysterious *okugi*, or arcana,

Famous Samurai: The Two Courts Period

## Nenami Okuyama Jion

of the Nen school of fencing. Among them were men like Tsutsumi Takarayama, Higuchi Tarō Kaneshige, and Kai Chikuzen no Kami. All of them were fencing masters in their own right, who went on to found their own schools of fencing.

This much, then, is known about the life and times of Nenami Jion and the way in which his school of fencing saw the light. It now seems almost a matter of historical negligence that in spite of his high birth and remarkable life, so very little is known about the man who stood at the cradle of the Nen-ryū and, through Nagahide's descendants, the Ittō-ryū of fencing. Yet this at times tantalizing paradox, too, can be ascribed to the treacherous murder of his father, Sōma Tadashige, master archer and one-time lord of the Fujigatani estate. Had the young Yoshimoto grown up as a normal warrior of the Shimōsa line of the Sōma clan, he would not have taken the tonsure at the age of seven, he would not have encountered the Chinese

*Opposite page*: A long flight of stairs leads to where once stood the Chōfuku temple

Even today practitioners pay homage to Jion's memory at the local nearby shrine

mercenary, and he would not have studied the art of Japanese fencing under Shinsō Eisuke. More likely, he would have become a master archer, in the tradition of his father and his father's father.

Having to salvage from the dim and blurred recesses of time the little that is recorded about this remarkable man seems a small price to pay for the legacy it helped to spawn. It is, after all, in that same flight into exile and that same secrecy of purpose that the young Yoshimoto found the inspiration and the ingredients for his life's achievement, the founding of the Nen-ryū, the first major and genuinely Japanese school of fencing.

It is almost to be expected that the greatest part of Jion's legacy was passed on to the following generations by his star pupil. What is remarkable, however, is that that student was already an old man by the time Jion took up the plan to build the Chōfuku temple. It was both a mark of Jion's generosity and of his pupil's winning talents, moreover, that their relationship ever came about, for the senior student whom Jion took into his confidence was none other than Chūjō Hyōgo no Kami Nagahide, scion of a clan that had served the Kamakura Bakufu for many generations.

# Nenami Okuyama Jion

## Principal characters in this chapter

| | |
|---|---|
| Ashikaga Tadayoshi: | Brother of Takauji and Bakufu general. |
| Ashikaga Takauji: | Chief general of the Northern Court and first shōgun of the Muromachi Bakufu. |
| Ashikaga Yoshimitsu: | The grandson of Ashikaga Takauji and third shōgun of the Muromachi Bakufu. |
| Chūjō Nagahide: | A pupil of Nenami and founder of the Chūjō-ryū. |
| Date Yukitomo: | Loyalist warlord from Hitachi. The lord of Isa castle, who joined Kitabatake Akiie on his last campaign to regain the capital. |
| Eda Yukiyoshi: | Commander in Nitta Yoshisada's army during the latter's western campaign. |
| Go-Daigo: | Emperor of the Southern Court. |
| Higuchi Kaneshige: | One of Nenami's pupils and founder of the Kaneshige Nen-ryū. |
| Hōjō Sadamasa: | General of the Kamakura Bakufu and governor of Musashi, who failed to halt Nitta Yoshisada in his march upon Kamakura. |
| Hōjō Takatoki: | Regent to the Kamakura Bakufu, and the man who sent Go-Daigo into exile. |
| Hōjō Yasuie: | General of the Kamakura Bakufu, and the man who managed to temporarily halt Nitta Yoshisada's march toward Kama-kura at Bubaigawara. |
| Horiguchi Sadamitsu: | Loyalist chieftain who joined Nitta Yoshisada when he raised banner of revolt at the Ikushina shrine. |
| Hosokawa Takamoto: | Commander of the Muromachi Bakufu who, together with Kakusa Kimisuke, intercepted Nitta Yoshisada near Fujishima castle. |
| Imagawa Sadayo: | Commissioner for Kyushu for the Muromachi Bakufu and leader of the campaign to crush the remnants of Loyalist resistance in Kyushu. |
| Ishido Yoshifusa: | Bakufu Constable in Izu and leader of the campaign against the Loyalists in the north. |

# Famous Samurai: The Two Courts Period

| | |
|---|---|
| Kakusa Kimisuke: | Commander of the Muromachi Bakufu who, together with Hosokawa Takamoto, intercepted Nitta Yoshisada near Fujishima castle. |
| Kaneyoshi, prince: | One of Go-Daigo's sons and leader of the Loyalist campaign following Kitabatake Chikafusa's death. |
| Kehi Ujiharu: | Loyalist warlord from Echizen. The lord of Kanagasaki castle. |
| Kitabatake Akiie: | First son of Kitabatake Chikafusa and leader of the Loyalist campaign in the north. |
| Kitabatake Akinobu: | Second son of Kitabatake Chikafusa, and the man who led the failed attempt to reestablish a Loyalist foothold in the north by recapturing Taga castle. |
| Kitabatake Chikafusa: | Strategist behind the Loyalist campaign. |
| Kō Morofuyu: | Son of Kō Moroyasu, and the general of the Muromachi Bakufu who joined Ishido Yoshifusa in his campaign against the Loyalists in the north. |
| Kō Moroyasu: | General of the Muromachi Bakufu, and the man routed by Nitta Yoshisada at Yahagi River and later by Uryū Tamotsu at the foot of Mount Somo. |
| Kōmyō: | Emperor of the Northern Court. |
| Kusunoki Masashige: | Loyalist warlord from Kawachi. Longtime adviser to Go-Daigo, and the man who died in the Battle at Minato River. |
| Miura Yoshikatsu: | Warlord from the Miura peninsula, who joined Nitta Yoshisada at Bubaigawara on his march against the Kamakura Bakufu. |
| Nitta Yoshiaki: | Son of Yoshisada who died during the fall of Kanagasaki castle. |
| Nitta Yoshisada: | The lord of Sōma Tadashige and leader of the Loyalist campaign. |
| Oda Haruhisa: | Loyalist warlord from Hitachi. Lord of Oda castle. |
| Ōdachi Muneuji: | Loyalist chieftain who joined Nitta Yoshisada when he raised the banner of revolt at the Ikushina shrine and died during the siege of Kamakura. |

| | |
|---|---|
| Ooida Ujitsune; | Commander in Nitta Yoshisada's army. |
| Oyama Hidetomo: | Loyalist warlord from Shimotsuke. Lord of Oyama castle, |
| Satomi Yoshitane: | Loyalist chieftain who joined Nitta Yoshisada when he raised the banner of revolt at the Ikushina shrine. |
| Satomi Yoshiuji: | Loyalist chieftain who failed to relieve Kanagasaki with support from Uryū Tamotsu. |
| Seki Munesuke: | Loyalist warlord from Hitachi. Lord of Seki castle. |
| Shiba Ienaga: | General of the Muromachi Bakufu who was routed by Kitabatake Akiie at Katase River and later fell en the defense of Kamakura. |
| Shiba Takatsune: | Constable in Echizen for the Muromachi Bakufu and leader of the siege of Kanagasaki castle. |
| Shimotsuma Masayasu: | Loyalist warlord from Hitachi. Lord of Taihō castle. |
| Shinsō Eisuke: | Warrior monk at the Jufuku temple in Kamakura under whom Nenami studied the art of fencing. |
| Sōma Chikatane: | (First son of Sōma Shigetane) Commander of the Muromachi Bakufu who joined Ishido Yoshifusa on his campaign against the Loyalists in the north and who was probably responsible for the death of Nenami's father, Sōma Tadashige. |
| Sōma Mitsutane: | (Second son of Sōma Shigetane) The man who built and later died in the defense of Odaka castle. |
| Sōma Morotane: | Founder of the Mutsu line of the Sōma clan. |
| Sōma Morotsune: | Ally of Minamoto Yoritomo in the Gempei War and founder of the Sōma clan. |
| Sōma Shigetane: | Bakufu commander and leader of the Mutsu line of the Sōma clan. |
| Sōma Tadashige: | Nenami's father and vassal to Nitta Yoshisada. |
| Sōma Tanemochi: | Nenami's younger brother. |
| Sōma Tanemura: | The last Sōma leader before the breakup of the clan into a Mutsu and Shimōsa line. |

# Famous Samurai: The Two Courts Period

| | |
|---|---|
| Sōma Taneuji: | Founder of the Shimōsa line of the Sōma clan. |
| Sugawara Michizane: | 9th century scholar-administrator and guardian diety of the Dazaifu Tenmangu. |
| Tsutsumi Takarayama: | One of Nenami's pupils. |
| Uryū Tamotsu: | Warlord from Echizen, and lord of Somoyama castle, who was persuaded by Wakiya Yoshisuke to fight for the Loyalist cause. |
| Utsunomiya Kintsuna: | Loyalist commander from Shimotsuke and lord of Utsunomiya castle, who had fought alongside Nitta Yoshisada at Takenoshita. |
| Wakiya Yoshisuke: | (Brother of Nitta Yoshisada) The man who joined Yoshisada on his western campaign and later on his flight into Echizen. |
| Yūki Chikatomo: | (Son of Yūki Munehiro) Lord of Shirakawa castle, and the man who failed to come to the aid of the Loyalists in the north. |
| Yūki Munehiro: | Loyalist warlord from Mutsu, and man who joined Kitabatake Akiie on his last, unsuccessful campaign to gain the capital. |

# CHŪJŌ NAGAHIDE

## Ono Takamura

The clan to which Nagahide belonged was an old clan, which traced its ancestry all the way back to the Heian period (857–1185). That period, which predated the periods of military rule, was one of great cultural achievement. The secret for that success lay in the period that preceded the Heian period, for already in the seventh century the Japanese court had come under the spell of the great imperial courts of China, the Sui and the Tang. Their shining example had led to the introduction of the Chinese script and had driven the Japanese lawmakers to reorganize the state along Chinese lines. Access to Chinese books had opened up to the Japanese artists, scholars, and lawmakers the immense amount of learning accumulated on the continents and they had learned fast and well.

Though on a much smaller scale, they had built a capital at Nara in the image of Chang'an, the capital both of the Sui and Tang empires. By then, sweeping reforms had been introduced that touched on almost every aspect of Japanese life, whether it be law, administration, military tactics, the arts, or religion. It was the urge to escape from the interference of the great Buddhist monasteries around Nara that made the administrators decide, in 793, to move the capital northward, toward the fertile basin that bordered the western shore of Lake Biwa. There, in the confluence of the Katsura and Kamo rivers, they began on the construction of Heian-kyō, an even larger copy of the great Chinese metropole. Heian-kyō, later renamed into Kyoto, was to remain the Japanese capital for more than a thousand years, until, early in the seventeenth century, the great unifier Tokugawa Ieyasu moved his seat of government to Edo.

The man to which Chūjō Nagahide and his clan members traced their ancestry was Ono Takamura, a courtier who lived during the ninth century, when the Heian court was at the height of its powers. Like his distant descendants, Takamura was a master horseman and archer, and standing six feet tall, he must have been a man who stood out from his contemporaries by his mere presence. Yet it is not so much for his martial as his literary accomplishments that Takamura was to become one of the few men of his time to leave a name for himself in the annals of Japanese ancient history, for he was one of the great Heian a poet-scholars.

In a society in which the arts were venerated almost as a religion, a man with Takamura's skills was greatly esteemed, and if we are to believe the ancient records, the poet scholar was a frequent guest at the court of the then emperor Saga. The emperor must have been impressed with the fruits of the poet's labors, for many of his waka have come down to us in imperial anthologies such as the *Shin kokinshū*. It must have been these, partly biographical, poems that helped preserve for posterity some of the more remarkable episodes of his eventful life, for the legends and tales around this extraordinary man are manifold.

Perhaps the best know among them is the tale of tragic love, recorded in the *Takamura monogatari*, or the Tale of Takamura. Its firs part, written roughly a century after Takamura's death, recounts how the courtier is hired as a Chinese tutor to his half-sister. Having hardly seen his half-sister before, but possessed of an amorous temperament, Takamura falls in love with the young woman at first sight. The latter at first objects at being instructed by her estranged half-brother, but it is not long before she returns his advances and becomes pregnant with his child. During one of their nightly trysts they are

Chūjō Hyōgo no Kami Nagahide

The Heian courtier Ono Takamura

overheard by her mother and barred from seeing each other ever again. Distraught and upset, she refuses all food and dies shortly thereafter. Takamura is broken-hearted, and though he eventually marries the daughter of a minister, he cannot forget his beloved half-sister, whose voice often comes to him in his dreams from the other side of the great divide—as on one occasion when, pining for his lost love, he spends the night in the vacant house that was once alive with her capturing presence and hears her whisper:

> Is this or is it not
> The man that I once knew?
> I cannot truly tell.
> Despite the one-time certainty
> Forget I never shall!

# Famous Samurai: The Two Courts Period

*Opposite page: Takamura gathers wood during his banishment on Oki Island*

Her death was not the only mishap to befall Takamura, and where the first blow fell in his private life the second blow was in the line of duty.

As a family of renowned scholars, the Ono had always been closely involved in the diplomatic exchanges between the Japanese and Chinese courts. It had been way back in 607 that Takamura's distant ancestor, Ono Imoko, was appointed as the head of the first official Japanese embassy to the court of the Sui dynasty. Shortly after that first mission, the Sui dynasty had been replaced by the Tang, but the exchanges had continued. Over the following centuries, many of Imoko's descendants had visited the continent in one official capacity or other. Recently, however, the unrest on the continent had increased and it had not been since 804 that an official mission had set sail for the continent. It was with some trepidation, then, that, in 833, Emperor Ninmyō decided to resume the exchanges with the people he and his predecessors had come to admire. He appointed Fujiwara Tsunetsugu to lead the mission, and since its main objective was to acquire Chinese books, paintings, and other artifacts, Takamura, with his vast knowledge of all things Chinese, was chosen to join him as deputy envoy.

Three more years it took before the embassy, comprising some six hundred men in all, finally sailed. But no sooner had it departed than it had to return home for repairs and renewed provisions. By the time the expedition was ready to sail again the relationship between the envoy and his deputy had soured to such an extent that Takamura excused himself on the grounds of poor health. It was granted, but being a man inclined to put his feelings into words, he could not refrain from writing a satirical poem on the folly of the mission. The emperor, already irritated by the scholar's withdrawal, failed to see the humor of the poem and ordered Takamura to be strangled. Upon appeal the sentence was commuted to banishment to a remote island, and in the autumn of 838, not long after Tsunetsugu had again sailed from Kyushu for China, Takamura departed from the port of Tottori to a life in exile on the island group of Oki.

The emperor soon began to miss the wit and piercing intelligence of the poet-scholar; within two years Takamura was allowed to return to the capital. The two years in exile had made a deep impression on Takamura, who, upon his return, took the tonsure and entered the Hōryū monastery.

Chūjō Hyōgo no Kami Nagahide

# Famous Samurai: The Two Courts Period

## Governor of Musashi

It was Ono Takayasu, one of Takamura's distant descendants, who, early in the tenth century, was appointed governor of the province of Musashi. The governor's seat, or Kokufu, was situated at Hachiōji, a small town in the shadow of Mount Takao, not far from Musashi's southern border with Sagami. There, on what are now the hallowed grounds of the Ōkunitama shrine, the nobleman from Kyoto began his new life as the representative of central government in Musashi.

Though most of Japan was nominally under central control, every now and then political stability was seriously upset by local revolts. Only a few decades before Takayasu had taken up his post as governor the famous rebel Taira Masakado had subdued eight of the eastern provinces, including Musashi, in a bid to become Japan's supreme ruler. Masakado's rebellion had

Chūjō Hyōgo no Kami Nagahide

The Ōkunitama shrine, built on the former site of the Musashi Kokufu

eventually been suppressed, but it was only with the help of local military leaders that central government in Kyoto was able to do so and continue their fragile hold on power.

Takayasu soon realized that he now found himself in the same situation. In the amorphous interlude of feeble central control that had followed the suppression of Masakado's rebellion, local warrior clans had asserted themselves. The clans descended from tribes that had lived in these fertile regions from time immemorial. They had sprung up as a nomadic people with no fixed abode, leading their herds from one valley to another, and living in close harmony with the seasons. With time they had settled in their favorite regions, living from the rice they grew in the fertile plains among the Kantō's many rivers. Their members had spread far afield, taking on the names of the regions that they had made their own. They were widely feared for their mastery of archery and horsemanship, and willing to make and break alliances whenever opportunity required them to do so.

85

# Famous Samurai: The Two Courts Period

Takayasu knew that, as a governor, he was the most senior representative of the imperial court in Kyoto. In theory, he had the authority to govern at will, yet without the necessary number of troops to enforce that will, he was as impotent as the lowest of officials. And thus, when, shortly after he had installed himself in his newly built residency, and the various representatives of the local power brokers came and went to subtly advocate wishes that might well become demands, the new governor could do little else than accommodate them as best he could.

Yet, even while he was building up his relations with the chieftains of the local warrior clans, Takayasu was putting into place the mechanisms for a more subtle means of control, founded on the old and trusted method of intermarriage. That method, the Fujiwara example had taught him, was the best method for a man in his position. Had the Fujiwara not, after all, managed to make even the once so mighty emperor a pliable tool in their wily hands, simply by having him marry their daughter? And thus he set about establishing ties with the local chieftains by marrying off his daughters to their sons, and having his own sons marry their daughters.

In a clan-based society, the new governor's strategy quickly bore fruit. His children produced many offspring and before long he had become the purveyor over a vast and intricate network of relationships with some of the most powerful local warrior houses. While in office, Takayasu drew on his authority as governor. After his retirement, he continued to build on the power base he had created and set about establishing his own clan.

So successful was Takayasu in his endeavors that by the end of the century the Ono could count themselves among the most powerful clans in the region. They possessed vast estates in the vicinity of Hachiōji and, through their network of relatives, controlled most of southern Musashi.

Like any great warrior clan, the Ono had all the trappings that came with military power. It was not yet an age in which warlords ensconced themselves in huge, fortified castles protected by garrisons. Instead they lived in large mansions, assembling in force whenever the occasion required them to fight. To celebrate and sustain the prosperity of the Ono name, Takayasu had a Shintō shrine erected on the southern bank of the Tama River, not far from where that mighty river was joined by the Asa River. That shrine, main-

# Chūjō Hyōgo no Kami Nagahide

The Ono *jinja*, the family shrine of the Ono clan

tained and patronized by the members of the Ono line until the present day, is still dedicated to the memory of, if perhaps not its most famous, then at least its most colorful member: the great poet-scholar Ono Takamura.

Upon his death at the turn of the tenth century, Takayasu was succeeded by his son, Yoshitaka, who moved the family seat to the vicinity of the Ono shrine. That area, located in the Tama district and famous for its beautiful cotton and silk fabrics, was known since ancient times as Tama no Yokoyama, the "mountains besides the Tama River." It was from this ancient name that Yoshitaka drew the name by which the members of his vast and influential family would be known: the Yokoyamadō, the House of Yokoyama. Henceforth Yoshitaka went by the name of Yokoyama no Taifu the "Great Leader of Yokoyama," the clan from which Chūjō Nagahide descended.

## Growing Power

For over a century Takayasu and his descendants dutifully served the imperial court in the capacity of governor of Musashi. Yet a lot had changed in the provinces since Takayasu had taken up that post. More and more it were the military chieftains and not the representatives of central government who dictated the course of local power politics. Some of them, such as Taira

## Famous Samurai: The Two Courts Period

Masakado's grandson, Tadatsune, had openly revolted, building the stronghold of Ōjii castle on the shore of Edo Bay, That revolt had been put down, and while it had not yet seriously threatened the authority of the court, it painfully revealed who were the real players on the political stage, for the rebel had been a member of the Taira clan, while the general sent down from Kyoto to subdue him had been a member of the Minamoto clan. Dazzled by the elevated splendor of the imperial court, both clans had thus far by and large submitted to central government, and in particular to the authority of the powerful Fujiwara regents. Yet in spite of the Fujiwara's prowess in the realm of politics the very status that made them feel that they were a cut above the rest was at the same time their Achilles heel. Those like the Fujiwara might belong to the court nobility, but in the implementation of their policies they invariably relied on the might of the military class.

It was almost inevitable, then, that in the enforcement of central policy much of the power and authority of central government devolved to the locally based warrior clans. It was a slow process, taking years to evolve, but all the more thorough and irrevocable for it.

This process was hastened in the case of local rebellions, for their suppression required huge military campaigns that, in turn, meant personal sac-

Minamoto Yorinobu lays siege to Ōji castle from the sea

rifices—sacrifices that had to be rewarded one way or the other. Since these were generally local disturbances, the court considered them the responsibility of the rural military chieftains, and was happy to let them decide on how to finance their campaigns and reward their allies. And thus the chieftains distributed among their vassals the estates they had fought so hard to conquer. So it had been with the Sōma when they had joined the Minamoto in the tough campaigns in the north, and so it was with dozens if not hundreds of other clans throughout the country.

It was different in the case of clans like the Ono. As a line of hereditary governors, they were required to represent the interests of the court as best they could. Yet the tradition of power politics among the tough and hardened warrior clans was a far cry from the effeminate world of the imperial court. With each year that passed, the court in Kyoto seemed more remote than ever, until at length its interests even clashed with those that served the Ono clan and the clans with which they had forged allegiances.

Within a few generations after Ono Takayasu had assumed the office of governor, the Yokoyamadō had become one of the most influential clans in Musashi. They were on a par with far older clans such as the Hirayama, the Inomata, and the Murayama. And while there were many more clans scattered throughout the hills and valleys of the province of Musashi, these were the most powerful. They were collectively known as the Musashi Nanadō, or "The Seven Houses of Musashi."

Among the clans that descended from the Yokoyamadō, the Narita had wandered farthest afield. One of Yoshitaka's sons, Ono Suketaka, had settled in the most northern regions of Mushashi, on a fertile stretch of land between the Ara and Tone rivers. The area was known by the name of Narita, and it was from here that Suketaka, in the image of his father, derived the name by which he would be known to his descendants, Narita no Taifu.

Suketaka was a successful chieftain, who belonged to some of the most trusted vassals of the Minamoto clan. His sons, too, were successful. Beside his eldest son, who inherited the leadership of the Narita, four of his other sons became chieftains in their own right. They founded their own clans, the Kodama, the Beppu, the Nara, the Tama-i, all named after the localities in which they had settled.

# Famous Samurai: The Two Courts Period

By this time, the Yokoyamadō were no longer the holders of the governorship of their province. That post had gone to Fujiwara Tsunemitsu, who was appointed governor of Musashi in 1132. Tsunemitsu was a descendant of the great Fujiwara Kamatari, the founder of the powerful clan of Heian regents. Like his predecessors Tsunemitsu chose to live in the province he governed. He had settled in the district of Chūjō, adopting its name as that by which his clan was to be known henceforth. His official residence, however, he had built on the outskirts of the nearby village of Kumagaya, an important post town along the Nakasendō. Whatever the motivations of the court were to appoint him, like Takayasu before him, Tsunemitsu found it impossible to govern the province without the close collaboration of the warrior houses. And thus, he, too, began to forge ties with the various chieftains to achieve his aims.

## A Warrior Clan

Little was now left of the ties that had bound the Ono to the imperial court. The various strands of the Yokoyamadō had fully integrated into the fabric of feudal society and had become a warrior clan in the best martial tradition. Only in their love of the arts and their emphasis on the pursuit of knowledge, whether it be architecture, administration, religion, or philosophy, did the Yokoyamadō stand out from the other warrior clans in the region. This did not mean that the latter had no eye for anything other than fighting—far from it. Ever since the first immigrants from the mainland had reached the shores of Japan, carrying among their few possessions the ancient scrolls of the Chinese sages, Chinese learning, and in particular the study of the Chinese classics had taken hold of the minds of the political, the religious, and the warrior classes alike. It was true that each of them did so for different reasons, but each had gained from the experience of that ancient and magnificent civilization. At court the bureaucrats studied the records of the Sui and Tang to learn how to organize their state efficiently and sustain it by the imposition of taxes. In the Buddhist temples monks poured over mandalas and other religious manuscripts recorded in the Chinese language in order

Chūjō Hyōgo no Kami Nagahide

The Chinese general-philosopher Sun Tzu

to gain a deeper understanding of their religion. On the field of battle the warriors put into practice the ancient tactics and strategies devised and tested long ago during the Chinese Warring States Period (403–221 BC). They carefully studied works like *The Art of War*, written by the great general-philosopher Sun Tzu.

Such was the influence of these teachings that Japanese chieftains took great pride in their application. Far from looking down on these foreign teachings, at each and every turn of events, whenever they faced new challenges, they strove to compare their predicament with those experienced by their Chinese heroes of ancient times. In doing so they stood to gain a lot, for where their Chinese heroes had only had the benefit of hindsight, after the experience of victory or defeat, they themselves could attain such in-

# Famous Samurai: The Two Courts Period

*Opposite page:* Minamoto Yoriyoshi, strikes a well with his bow during the northern campaign

sights even before they went into battle. Nor did the Japanese chroniclers make any effort to disguise the continental influences that lay behind some of the successes on the Japanese field of battle. Even in the *Taiheiki*—a work recorded during the second half of the fourteenth century, when Japan already boasted a martial tradition of many centuries—they do not fail to do so. It is almost with relish that they seize the opportunity to remind their audiences of the great Chinese examples when, in their description of the second clash between the Loyalist forces of Nitta Yoshisada and those of the Kamakura Bakufu in the Battle at Kotesashi, they recount how:

> The sixty thousand warriors from Kamakura formed one body, spreading out in an attempt to encircle the enemy. Seeing this, Yoshisada's warriors formed themselves into a wedge, so that their center would not collapse. Thus the two armies clashed, since all warriors know of Huang Shih Kung's way of binding a tiger, and all know Chang Tzu-fang's way of crushing a devil.

The many members of the Yokoyamadō needed no such reminding. They had been raised and trained on a constant diet of the Chinese classics and were deeply imbued with these ancient tenets of warfare.

Due to their noble origins the members of the Yokoyamadō had largely adhered to the policies that emanated from the imperial court. They had experienced at close quarters the lasting effects that local rebellions had had on the region, and were the first to help in their suppression, as, for instance, in 1062, when Narita Suketaka had responded to the call for assistance of Minamoto Yoriyoshi in the suppression of the Emishi. Legend has it that, on his way to Dewa, Yoriyoshi had called on Suketaka and that during that visit he had lent his bow and sword to the village elder in order to kill a huge snake that had made a nearby pond its home. The incredible hardships suffered during the harsh winter campaigns in the northern province had forged a special bond between the Narita and the Minamoto. That bond was tried and tested on more campaigns over the following decades, so that the ties between the Minamoto and the various strands of the Yokoyamadō grew increasingly close over the next century. It was a lord-vassal relationship that

## Chūjō Hyōgo no Kami Nagahide

required huge sacrifices from men like Suketaka, yet he and his fellow chieftains served their overlord well. The Minamoto, after all, though they demanded absolute loyalty, knew how to reward their vassals for their long years of service. They also were a clan on the rise, whose leaders were often seen at court and whose ever expanding estates throughout the Kantō were palpable proof of the power they exercised.

The Yokoyamadō stood to gain a lot, then, from such a powerful alliance, and given that the increasing power of their overlords was sanctioned by the court they need not fear that their own longstanding commitment to the state was being compromised. All that was to change dramatically toward the middle of the twelfth century, when the members of the Yokoyamadō were finally forced to choose between their ancient yet deeply felt commitments to an aloof and distant court and their longstanding ties of loyalty to a generous yet demanding lord.

## A Growing Rivalry

The Minamoto were not the only clan to dominate the military landscape of the Heian period; there were other powerful clans that competed with them for influence at court. The most powerful among these were the Taira. Both the Minamoto and the Taira were of imperial descent, and both had established their local power base after being appointed by the court as governors or vice-governors. They had spread throughout the eastern and western provinces, although they were both most numerous in the east. There the descendants of the Taira (including the Chiba and the Sōma) even outnumbered those of the Minamoto, but it were the latter who had become the most powerful clan in the Kantō. In the west it was different; there the Taira were still free to grow and widen their sphere of influence without having to submit or pander to the whims of what were in essence their chief rivals. This, incidentally, was exactly what happened, and it seems one of those remarkable ironies of history that the ascendancy of the western Taira was made possible by an almost exact reverse of events that had given the Minamoto such powers in the east.

## Chūjō Hyōgo no Kami Nagahide

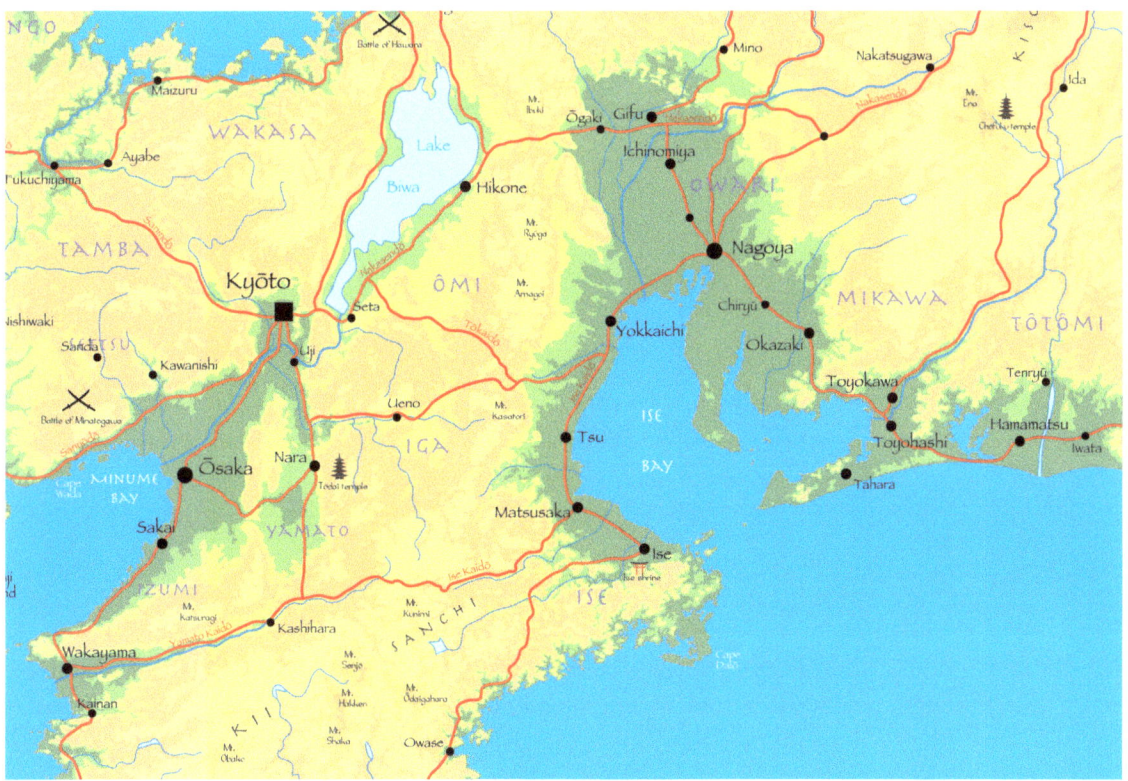

One of the many warriors of Taira descent had settled in the province of Ise. That had been at the turn of the eleventh century, when a certain Taira Korehira was appointed as the province's governor. Largely by the same methods and mechanisms by which the Ono had consolidated their power base in Musashi, the Taira managed to entrench themselves into their new surroundings. By the end of the century, they controlled not only the province they had been appointed to govern, but also large tracts of land in the neighboring province of Iga. In their home province of Ise they had been able to do so through the steady encroachment upon the lands that had originally belonged to the Shrine of Ise. In Iga they did the same with those of the Tōdai temple in Nara.

Yet despite their wealth, their vast estates, the influence of the western Taira remained only marginal at court. There, it was the Minamoto who held sway among the political elite. It had been the Minamoto, after all, who had

# Famous Samurai: The Two Courts Period

Minamoto Yoshiie, undisputed hero of the northern campaigns

subdued the rebellious eastern—Taira—chieftains, first the legendary Masakado and then his grandson, Tadatsune. Indeed, so fearful had the latter been of the Minamoto reputation that he had surrendered without a fight. Tadatsune had died shortly afterward, but his sons had become Minamoto vassals. All that had been long ago, but it had so firmly established the military reputation of the Minamoto that it remained unchallenged throughout the tenth and eleventh centuries. That reputation was reaffirmed by their successes in the northern campaigns, and the Taira watched with envy how, in the wake of all these successes, the prestige of the Minamoto at court continued to grow. Perhaps the greatest among the Minamoto warriors was Yoshiie, the hero of the second campaign in the north, who was considered by all to be the *tenka daiichi buyū no shi*, "the foremost military hero in the realm." By the descendants of his own clan he was revered as Hachiman Tarō, the firstborn of Hachiman, the God of War. What the western Taira needed was a chance to display their own military prowess, their loyalty to the court, and their superiority over their eternal rivals.

It must have been with some delight that, at the turn of the twelfth century, the leaders of the Ise Taira first heard of the depredations of a certain Minamoto chieftain in the south, a governor, no less, who had gravely upset the court by his misrule. That delight must have turned into ecstasy when they learned that that very same governor was Minamoto Yoshichika, the son of the undisputed hero of the northern campaigns, Yoshiie.

# Decline of the Minamoto

It seems that even the leaders of the Minamoto had had their doubts about the political qualities of Yoshichika. It had been on their advice, after all, that, in 1101, the court had appointed the young warrior as the governor of Tsushima. It seemed a prudent decision, as Tsushima, an island off the western coast of Kyushu, lay far away from the home provinces, where his erratic behavior might do much damage. Yet it was not long after his appointment that ominous tidings began to reach the capital. The court's representatives at the Dazaifu reported that the new governor of Tsushima was committing outrages. They complained that he was suppressing the people and that he was using the revenues that belonged to the state to pay his motley gang of thugs, thieves, and murderers. Greatly distraught by the blemish his son's actions might cast on the family name, Yoshiie immediately decided to take the matter in hand and sent one of his senior vassals down to Kyushu to bring the prodigal son back into the family fold. The vassal never reported back and after several months of anxious waiting the august but aging warrior had to learn that his envoy, too, had joined the rebellious ranks of his wayward son. Moreover, Yoshichika had landed at Hakata and had made the Dazaifu into his new headquarters from where to terrorize the surrounding provinces with impunity. For some time the court ignored the actions of the rebellious governor, but when he committed the offense of murdering a local government official who sought to deal with him, they sent down a large force and banished him to the island of Oki. Peace had been restored to the southern provinces, but the political damage had been done.

Over the next few years, his final years, Yoshiie had to observe how the prestige of the Minamoto at court steadily declined. Had it merely been out of fear that he had been respected? It certainly seemed so, for he felt that his contribution to the state had never been fully appreciated. He remembered

# Famous Samurai: The Two Courts Period

## Chūjō Hyōgo no Kami Nagahide

well how, midway on his return from the second northern campaign in the province of Mutsu, news reached him that the court had decided not to recompense him for the immense financial costs he had incurred, as they considered the rebels he had fought his "private enemies." It was only logical, they had argued, that private enemies should be fought with private funds. In anger he had flung the heads of the rebels, which he had hoped to present to the court on his arrival in the capital, into a ditch along the road. This was all perfectly legal, as the court's decision had made them his private property, and he could dispense of them as he liked, but it did little to alleviate the outrage he had felt at the court's ingratitude. They had even had the audacity to take away again his governorship of Mutsu, forcing him to pay his vassals out of the revenues from his family's old properties in the Kantō. Now, due to his son's depredations, many of these, too, were confiscated, so that he was reduced to a state of dependency. Thus he lived out his final years, a ruined, humiliated, and deeply embittered warrior, revered by his own class, but looked down upon by an ungrateful court.

Yoshiie did not live to see the next year, when news reached the capital that his son had escaped from Oki island. The reports were vague, but it was clear that Yoshichika had landed at Matsumoto and had resumed his old career of murder and pillage in the province of Izumo. The news also reached the headquarters of the Taira clan in Ise, and their fervent hopes were answered when Taira Masamori, at that time the governor of the neighboring province of Inaba, was appointed by the court as *tsuitōshi*, the general in charge of the punitive force to bring the outlaw to heel. It was a remarkable stroke of good luck, for the initial choice of the court had fallen on Yoshiie's eldest son, Yoshimune. The latter, however, had extricated himself from this onerous duty on the excuse that he and his brother had once solemnly sworn never to become each other's enemies.

Seizing his chance, Masamori set about his duties with vigor and decorum. On February 2, 1108, on the morning of his departure, he rode up to the residence of Yoshichika, shot several arrows at the outlaw's mansion, drew his sword, and hewed a number of deep gashes into the main gate. All this was strictly in accordance to custom, but to some of the older bystanders it seemed that something in the almost perfunctory way in which the ritual

*Opposite page:* Minamoto Yoshiie, unable to stop the decline of his clan

# Famous Samurai: The Two Courts Period

Taira Masamori enters the capital with Yoshichika's head

was executed did not ring wholly true. It somehow lacked the fierceness and intensity of purpose of proven warriors such as the great Yoshiie. The general mood in the capital, however, was one of excitement—an excitement that poured over into a state of jubilant exultation when, a month later, on March 3, Masamori entered the capital's wide avenues in a grand procession, carrying with him the head of Minamoto Yoshichika. A diarist who observed the spectacle noted how the culprit's head:

> was impaled on a pike and carried by five serving men, flanked on each side by forty or fifty foot soldiers, armed and in full armor, and followed by Masamori and one hundred of his retainers, their swords and spears glittering in the sunshine.

The court must at least have shared some of the exasperation of the Taira leaders with the military prestige of the Minamoto, for it was with unprecedented alacrity that Emperor Shirakawa appointed the upstart chieftain to governor of the first-rank province of Tajima, a post that had not even been occupied by Minamoto Yoshiie.

Some had suspected from the outset that more was at work than a genuine rejoicing at the capture of an enemy of the state. They recalled how they had raised their brows when, within only weeks of his departure from the capital, Masamori had sent word that he had already seized the culprit. They recalled their utter astonishment when, even prior to Masamori's return and the presentation of solid proof, the emperor had announced the promotion that awaited Masamori on his return. Now it dawned on them that the whole thing might have been an elaborate scheme, devised by the court to rid itself of the powerful Minamoto.

Rumors began to surface that the head sent down from Izumo was not at all that of the great warrior, but that of a poor peasant, callously sacrificed in the service of the Taira campaign for the court's favor. They really took hold when, not long after Masamori's appointment, they were fuelled by repeated reports from the provinces that Yoshichika had been sighted, alive and well, happily pursuing his old habits with his band of rebels. The Taira tried hard to combat these rumors, but the more they did so, the more the people loved them. As many as four expeditions were launched over the next few years to catch the rebel, each claiming the same result as the first one, and each presenting the same gruesome evidence. The rumors, of course, persisted. Instead of dying, they grew into elaborate folk tales about rebels with five lives and five-headed men.

Whatever the truth behind the rumors, the tales, and the sightings, even to the more level-headed observer it seemed that a combination of Masamori's fame and Yoshichika's infamy had brought to naught all the hard campaigning of the Minamoto throughout the previous two centuries. Gone were the glorious tales of how Minamoto Tsunemoto had tracked down Taira Masakado and his fellow rebels and sent their heads to the capital for inspection. Gone the gleeful accounts of the humility with which Taira Tadatsune had submitted to the authority of Minamoto Yorinobu. And gone the long-spun tales of Yoshiie's incredible feats of heroism amid the long and cold winters of the northern provinces—all seemed to have evaporated overnight. It was enough to make even the most cynical and disinterested man shake his head in disbelief over the fickle nature of humankind and the ingratitude of courtiers. To the proud and ever loyal Minamoto it was simply unbearable. What had they done to lose the favor of the court within such a short time-span? How could such a nondescript upstart from the west have risen to such heights with so little effort? How could they redeem their honor, and when would the opportunity present itself to do so?

## Rise of the Taira

Whether Taira Masamori's appointment was the result of a conspiracy between his clan and the court or whether it was attributable solely to his valor, his actions resulted in the unstoppable ascendancy of the Taira clan from the turn of the twelfth century onward. Within years of his appointment, Masamori could count himself at least an equal to the Minamoto chieftains. Whenever they were called upon to stand guard at one of the court's many functions, so was Taira Masamori, the man who only years before had been no more than a local warrior of no political consequence.

One of the secrets behind his success was his unquestionable ability to play up to the people's desire for spectacle. As in 1119, when he led another great procession through the streets of the capital. This time he had seized a large number of pirates and bandits who had been terrorizing the coastal regions of the western provinces. It must have been the bad experience with Minamoto Yoshichika's elusive head that caused him to change a few details in the program, for this time he had generously decided to postpone the execution of the criminals until after the event, anxious to show to the people that he had not only caught the heads that had conceived the crimes, but also the bodies that had perpetrated them. The cynically inclined thought otherwise. They argued that he had spared the lives of the criminals so as to recruit them for his considerable seagoing force. The show nevertheless had the desired effect, for that same year Masamori was promoted yet again, this time to the meteoric heights of fourth retainer. So spectacular was Masamori's rise to fame that it was said that even the usually so credulous populace "could not believe their eyes and ears."

It would be unfair to suggest that the Taira ascendancy was based on nothing but hot air. Far from it. Like their eastern counterparts, the Ise Taira

## Chūjō Hyōgo no Kami Nagahide

Taira Masamori engages with *akuso* just south of the capital

were warriors of great ability. Long before Masamori's successes, they had built up a reputation for the effective way with which they dealt with piracy and brigandage. Of that there was much around, for the countryside during the Heian period was far from peaceful. There was hardly a province that was not in some degree afflicted by the depredations of whole companies of roving bandits or marauding pirates, and it was only with the help of the powerful rural warrior houses like the Taira that order was restored and that central authority was maintained. Even the capital itself was not free from these scourges, although here it was the *akusō*, the bands of "bad monks" belonging to rival Buddhist sects, who were behind the unrests. These precursors to the later *sōhei*, would frequently clash on the streets of the capital and cause general mayhem. Their mutual disputes had started on the ground of doctrinal differences, but once the chief abbots had tasted the intoxicating effects of military power they soon organize the *akusō* into permanent fighting squads, deployed to intimidate the court into complying with their extortionist demands. By the turn of the twelfth century the sects had become so powerful that even the imperial guard was unable to keep them in check,

# Famous Samurai: The Two Courts Period

*Opposite page*: Taira Tadamori shocks the court by drawing his sword

forcing the court to call in the help of the military. And here, too, Masamori played a valuable role, for it was with his help that, in the spring of 1113, Minamoto Tameyoshi managed to quell a rebellion of the Enryaku temple's Tendai sect.

Nor were these qualities limited to just one generation of the Taira clan. Masamori's son, Tadamori, continued to build on his family's successes. Like his father, he was a shrewd political operator, who did not shy away from bending the instruments of government to suit his own needs, as in 1133, when he drafted a forged official document forbidding Song merchant ships to conduct trade with the court's representatives in Dazaifu. Hakata and the other Kyushu ports at which they called, he argued, fell under the jurisdiction of the governor of Hizen. Consequently, they were to submit their wares to him for "official examination" as he was the person who happened to occupy that post.

Tadamori was only able to get away with such outrages by plying the court and keeping on intimate terms with the retired Emperor Toba, for whom he built a large Buddhist hall. In reward, he was made a courtier with the right to attend upon the emperor. This, of course, greatly upset the other courtiers, and it was not long before some of them conspired to rid themselves of the intruder. Being a warrior with a warrior's instinct, Tadamori sensed the hostilities and took the necessary precautions. The *Heike monogatari* recounts in vivid detail how, invited to a banquet, the warrior brought with him a large dagger, hiding it in the long sleeves of his court robes. At one stage during the evening, when he knew he had the full attention of all the participants, he moved toward the faint light of a chamber lamp, and slowly but deliberately drew the long weapon from his sleeve and held it next to his head, "its blade gleaming like ice."

It seemed a symbolic threshold had been crossed. Never before had a courtier been allowed to enter the palace grounds carrying a weapon without the explicit permission of the emperor. Not only had Tadamori flouted this injunction, he had even had the nerve to bring along a retainer, whom he had put on guard in the adjacent garden, ready to rush to his aid when called for. It was true that the evening had drawn to a close without further incident; on his departure, Tadamori had entrusted the weapon to one of the

## Chūjō Hyōgo no Kami Nagahide

palace's a female attendants. Asked by his retainer, he had casually remarked that "nothing much had happened." His views were not shared by the other courtiers. Secretly outraged at the blatancy with which Tadamori had countered their subterfuge, they publicly fulminated at the committed offense and demanded that his name be removed from the duty-board. Even the emperor, who, like his predecessor, had showered the Taira clan with imperial favors, was disturbed by the news. But when Tadamori was called in for questioning he quickly defused the situation by calling for the female attendant to whom he had entrusted his weapon. When, on the emperor's request, she produced the weapon, it turned out to be made of lacquered wood, its blade covered with silver paper. Tadamori had never been in breech of palace regulations, and it was with some relief that the emperor pardoned the warrior for his "jest."

Tadamori, meanwhile, was satisfied that his sinister gesture was understood by all who had been present. However superior the Heian nobility might feel to the warrior class, however crude and boorish his manners might seem when compared to their refined and cultivated ways, they were deeply mistaken if they thought that they could outwit him at his own game. Let them make fun of his provincial upbringing and deride his poor skills at dancing and poetry, they better get used to the idea that the courtiers were not the only ones who could move in the emperor's shadow. Such, then, was the cunning of Taira Tadamori, but even he was outshone by his son and heir, Kiyomori, the man destined to play such a central role in events that were to lead to the demise of the Fujiwara and the permanent rise of the military.

# The Hōgen Insurrection

When Tadamori died in 1153, he was succeeded by his son, Kiyomori. The young warrior had many of the qualities of his father and grandfather. Like his father he continued to push the trade with Song China, thereby greatly increasing the wealth and prestige of the Taira clan. Using his wealth, he undertook the construction of impressive buildings, such as the Sanjūsangendō, the Monastery of the thirty-three bays, situated in the Higashiyama area, just

## Chūjō Hyōgo no Kami Nagahide

The Sanjūsangendō

east of the capital. On its completion it was furnished with one thousand and one statues of Kannon, the goddess of mercy. Measuring over one hundred meters in length, it was Japan's longest wooden structure. Such feats of ostentation greatly facilitated his acceptance at court, something at which his father had never really succeeded and had worked even harder for to realize for his son. Kiyomori's close contact with the nobility from an early age had endowed him with a refinement and a sense of taste required in those whose lives were played out on the national stage. Being raised in close proximity to the court, where everything moved at a slow pace, he had also learned to shed some of the warrior's temper and to bide his time.

For all his talents, efforts, and good breeding (his mother had once been the favorite concubine of the retired Emperor Shirakawa), Kiyomori was far from achieving his ultimate ambition of absolute control. Many were the hurdles that needed to be taken before he could even consider that goal ac-

## Famous Samurai: The Two Courts Period

complished, and perhaps the biggest hurdle was posed by the Minamoto. For the moment the Taira might enjoy the emperor's favor, but the sympathies of Emperor Go-Shirakawa were notoriously fickle, and they might easily drift elsewhere. Or they might again be bestowed on the Minamoto, who were still a force to be reckoned with. As their suppression of the two great Taira rebellions in the Kantō had shown, their control over Japan's eastern provinces remained unchallenged. For the time being they had taken a backseat, perhaps even preferring to do so in order to address dissension within their own ranks, but the Taira warrior knew all too well that the Minamoto were a proud clan, who needed little incentive to pounce on him, especially if they could thereby redress the ignominies they had been made to endure as a result of his father's actions.

Kiyomori still had a long way to go before he could claim true ascendancy over his military rivals, and longer still before he could aspire to the kind of sway over the imperial family held by the Fujiwara regents. For more than two centuries their hold on political power had been nearly absolute. It was true that since Emperor Go-Sanjō (1034–1073) the imperial house had managed to curtail the influence of the Fujiwara. They had done so by the ingenious system of "cloister government," by which an emperor would retire,

Taira Kiyomori, working tirelessly for his clan's ascendancy

take the tonsure, and dictate the affairs of state from his spiritual retreat. But among the many courtiers who vied for influence, the position of the Fujiwara remained unchallenged, It seemed auspicious, not only to Kiyomori, but to all those who craved the kind of influence enjoyed by the Fujiwara, then, when a succession dispute arose within the wall of the imperial palace itself. Such disputes, after all, required all factions with a degree of influence or interest in the affairs of state to choose sides. It was always a gamble, but if the Fujiwara happened to end up on the losing side, it must certainly mean that the Taira had to be on the side of those who would win.

As always, succession disputes were complicated matters. When Emperor Toba retired he had, as custom required, crowned his first son, Sutoku, emperor. Shortly afterward, however, one of his concubines, the daughter of a Fujiwara, bore him a son. He was so taken with the boy that he forced the young Sutoku to retire and made his newborn, Konoe, then still only three years old, emperor. But the young boy had a weak constitution, and he died at the age of seventeen. The whole realm now expected Sutoku's son, Shigehito, to ascend the throne, but it was not to be, for in that same year Sutoku's younger brother, Go-Shirakawa, was chosen as the new emperor. Sutoku, who had come to terms with his forced retirement, was rightfully outraged that his son was being passed over. Shortly after Go-Shirakawa's appointment he left the seclusion of the Tanaka Hall at Toba and took up residence at the Shirakawa Palace, on the eastern embankment of the Kamo River. There he was visited with increasing frequency by all manner of men unsympathetic to the new emperor, and before long rumors were about that he was preparing to seize the throne for his son by force.

It soon transpired that one of the men who were in collusion with Sutoku was Fujiwara Yorinaga. Yorinaga had been a promising young courtier, who had risen to prominence by being appointed *nairan*, or personal assistant, to the infant emperor Konoe. He was a man of exceptional abilities, a great scholar, well versed in language and history, and an able administrator. No one had doubted that he would become the tutor of the newly appointed emperor, and great was the consternation when, shortly after the installation of the new emperor, the camp of Go-Shirakawa made it known that they had appointed someone else to become the imperial tutor. It must have been

# Famous Samurai: The Two Courts Period

*Opposite page*: A sinister Emperor Sutoku invokes a thunderstorm

their shared sense of injustice that drew these two able men together, for it was not long after these events that Yorinaga became a frequent visitor of Sutoku's new quarters of Shirakawa palace. There, in great secrecy, they worked on their plans on how they might rid themselves of Go-Shirakawa and his followers and put Sutoku's son to the throne. To help them in that effort, Yorinaga had sent out word to sympathetic chieftains, urging them to converge on the capital and rally around the unrightfully deposed emperor. It was the interception and interrogation of a group of such warriors at the barrier on the capital's southern outskirts by one of Kiyomori's sons, the seventeen-year-old Motomori, that the plot was exposed and that the imperial palace, too, began to make preparations for the standoff that must inevitably follow.

The news from his son that Yorinaga had chosen the side of the retired emperor filled Kiyomori with promise and it was with great eagerness that he responded to an imperial summons to rally behind the newly installed emperor. His enthusiasm was somewhat dampened when, on his arrival at the imperial palace, he found that a large number of Minamoto chieftains had rallied behind Go-Shirakawa. It was true that the clan elder, Minamoto Tameyoshi, together with six of his sons had chosen the side of Sutoku. But Tameyoshi was by now an old man. Unlike his father, the great Yoshiie, he had little experience of fighting, nor did he exert the kind of control over his clan his father had done. This was evident in the number of Minamoto who had rallied behind the new emperor. Among them were up-and-coming chieftains such as Minamoto Yorimasa, the son of Tadamasa, the governor of Settsu. Or Minamoto Yoshiyasu, the son of Tameyoshi's cousin, Yoshikuni. Greatest proof of the old man's weakening hold on his clan was the presence in the Go-Shirakawa camp of his eldest son, Yoshitomo.

Unlike his father, who had spent most of his life in the capital, Yoshitomo had been raised in the garrison town of Kamakura and had led the life of a warrior. Under his young but talented leadership the clan had subdued large parts of Mikawa and Shimōsa and thereby managed to sustain the material legacy of the great Hachiman Tarō, Yoshiie. Kiyomori knew that it were men such as Yoshitomo who posed the greatest obstacle to his ambitions, and their impressive presence at the imperial palace seriously foreshortened any

# Chūjō Hyōgo no Kami Nagahide

## Famous Samurai: The Two Courts Period

chances that the me might emerge as the sole winner from this imperial dispute. For the moment, however, the immediate threat came from the other side of the Kamo River, for it was still far from certain whether the camp of the new emperor would emerge victorious.

On the eve of July 29, 1156, the first year of the Hōgen era, the odds between the two opposing forces were evenly distributed and in both camps the ringleaders were heatedly deliberating on what course of action to take. The most experienced warrior in the Sutoku camp was Tameyoshi's eighth son, the young Tametomo. Due to the young man's fierce disposition his father had sent him down to Kyushu, where he had made a name for himself by bringing as many as nine provinces under Minamoto control. He had subdued many a stronghold on his campaigns, and he proposed that they attack the palace of Go-Shirakawa that very night, before his eldest brother would do the same to them. This plan was rejected out of hand by Yorinaga, who derided the southerner for his provincial notions about warfare. Burning an imperial residence was not the way in which one conducted war at the nation's center of power. The courtier insisted that they wait until the next day when they would be joined by sympathetic *sōhei* from the Kōfuku monastery in Nara.

Minamoto (on horseback) Tametomo defends the Shirakawa palace

Intimidated by the aura of a member of the court nobility Tametomo did not argue with Yorinaga, but to himself he mused that such matters should be left to fighting men. He knew that Yoshitomo, too, was a warrior well versed in the stratagems of war. If Yoshitomo were to advance that same night and start fires upwind, they would be trapped like mice.

Thus the ignorance of the arrogant courtier won out over the experience of the humble warrior. And thus Yorinaga sealed the fate of all those who had rallied behind the retired emperor. For that night Yoshitomo's and Kiyomori's men attacked in great force, driving Tametomo and his men back on the defensive. For several hours they managed to hold out in the face of superior forces, and only when Yoshitomo ordered his men to start fires upwind was the Sutoku camp forced to make their escape and abandon the Shirakawa palace. Tameyoshi, his sons, and the retired emperor escaped to temporary safety, but Yorinaga was struck by an arrow in the neck and died before he and his followers had reached the safety of Saga.

# Retribution

At least for Minamoto Yoshitomo the suppression of the Hōgen Insurrection, so named after the era in which it occurred, felt like the first step on the road to recovery. Though the Taira had played an important role, it had been Minamoto warriors who had won the day for the sitting emperor. As his younger brother had feared, Yoshitomo had indeed decided on a surprise attack. Early that morning, under cover of dusk, he and Kiyomori had left the imperial palace and set out eastward along the second main thoroughfare (Nijō). When they reached the Kamo River, Kiyomori had crossed the river at the third main thoroughfare (Sanjō), from where he rode northward. His troops were the first to see serious action, but when their advance guard was repelled by Tametomo and his men, they retreated. Warned by Kiyomori's setback, Yoshitomo, who had followed the river's western riverbed, ordered his men to attack in full force. They, too, were at first repelled, but eventually managed to drive Tametomo back toward the palace, where, for the next few hours, they engaged the enemy at close quarters.

# Famous Samurai: The Two Courts Period

Minamoto Tametomo (now on foot) holds out on the balcony of the Shirakawa palace

Among them were warriors of great repute, men such as Chiba Tsunetane and Chiba Hirotsune, whose clan had been allied to Minamoto ever since their ancestor Taira Tadatsune had submitted to the authority of Minamoto Yorinobu. There had been great warrior chieftains from the other provinces, from Mino, Mikawa, Ito, Sagami, Shimōsa, Kazusa, and Awa, but most of them were from the province of Musashi.

Just how great a service the Musashi warriors had rendered to the sitting emperor is borne out by the *Hōgen monogatari*, the riveting tale of the events of the Hōgen Insurrection. Listing the many eastern warriors who fought on the side of Yoshitomo, the chroniclers make special mention of the members of the Musashi Nanadō who took part in the fighting at the Shirakawa palace: the Hirayama, the Kodama, the Murayama, the Inomata, and, not to forget, the powerful Yokoyama. Indeed, so fiercely did the warriors of the Yokoyama clan fight that the chroniclers went out of their way to record their bravery:

Chūjō Shingo and Shinroku, Narita no Tarō, Hakota no Jirō, Nara no Saburō, Iwagami no Tarō, Beppu no Jirō, Tamai no Shirō, and those below them threw themselves into the melee, taking turns in advancing and doing battle. Each and every one of them took heads and when they retreated after all of them had been wounded, a warrior in armor laced with black leather, wearing a helmet with high antlers, and riding a grey steed, announced himself as Akushichi Bettō [the elder brother of Tametomo] and dashed forward. Ebina Gempachi spurred on his horse and engaged him, but when he was shot in his armor skirt and recoiled, Saitō Bettō Sanemori immediately drew up beside him, upon which Akushichi Bettō drew his long sword and struck the bowl of Sanemori's helmet. Sanemori, in spite of being struck, planted the tip of his sword in the former's helmet and drove it home, causing Akushichi's head to fall inevitably forward. Picking up the head and impaling it on the tip of his sword, Sanemori raised it aloft and called out: "I am Saitō Bettō Sanemori, descendant in the seventeenth generation of Shōgun Toshihito, resident of the province of Musashi, thirty-one tears of age, and this is how I do battle!"

Yet in spite of all the bravery and selfless sacrifice of Yoshitomo and his men, Emperor Go-Shirakawa failed to honor their contribution in the way they had expected. Only Yoshitomo was promoted, but even he was only raised to the position of Acting Chief of the Left Division of the Horse Bureau. When, on top of this, the emperor's favorite, Kiyomori, who had seen little action, was promoted to governor of Harima, Yoshitomo exploded. He indignantly pointed out that, in direct contravention to the dictates of filial piety, he had opposed his father and abandoned his brothers. Moreover, he had even fought with them and sought to take their lives out of reverence for the emperor. On hearing this, the court was put to shame and quickly raised his rank from acting to that of active chief.

Yoshitomo had gained in rank in return for his loyalty to the sitting emperor, but only in the wake of the revolt did he truly come to understand the terrible price his clan had payed for him having defied his father's will. The old Tameyoshi had taken refuge in the house of a friend in the nearby town of Sakamoto. Not long after, he fell gravely ill and decided to return to the capital and put his fate in the hands of the court, hoping that his son Yoshitomo, if not able to save the life of his wayward father, would at least

## Famous Samurai: The Two Courts Period

secure an amnesty for his brothers, all of whom had obeyed their father's will and joined the insurgents.

By then, a most gruesome precedent had been set in the administering of retributions. Kiyomori's uncle, Tadamasa, together with his four sons had been the only chief members of the Taira clan to choose the side of the retired emperor. They, too, had made their escape on the morning of July 29. By way of refuge, the old warrior had taken the tonsure. He had entered a monastery in the Jōdo Valley, at the western foot of Mount Hiei, not far from where Tameyoshi had been hiding. The news that Tameyoshi had given himself up to his son instilled hopes in the old warrior that he might also be pardoned, and thus he sent word to Kiyomori that he and his sons were willing to return to the capital and put their lives in his hands. It was a fateful error, for the unscrupulous Kiyomori was more concerned with the destruction of the Minamoto than the fate of his fellow clan members. He argued the court

Mount Hiei, where many of the rebels had gone into hiding

would be incapable of showing any leniency toward the old Tameyoshi and his sons if he, Kiyomori, dealt otherwise with the wayward members of his own clan. And thus he arranged to meet Tadamasa and his sons outside the capital, on the western bank of the Kamo River, well away from the prying eyes of any unwanted onlookers. There, in the riverbed of the capital's majestic waterway, he had the fugitives arrested and tied. He first put to death his uncle and then his four nephews, young warriors in the prime of life, with whom he had grown up and fought his first battles. Now he found himself severing their heads—severing the sacred ties that had bound them together as a clan—simply so as to set the horrible precedent by which the events of the following days must inevitably unfold.

It was left to the wretched Yoshitomo to play his tragic role in the cunning plan of his professed ally. It had been more than three centuries since capital punishment had been meted out to men who had threatened to dethrone the emperor, but no amount of petitioning on Yoshitomo's part could induce Go-Shirakawa to show any leniency. And thus Yoshitomo set in motion the wheels by which he would commit the worst of the Five Abominable Crimes in the Buddhist scripture: to kill one's own father.

Yoshitomo had not the courage himself either to murder or even to break the news to his father. Instead, he sent out henchmen to intercepted Tameyoshi's palanquin at one of the capital's many intersections and take the old man's life. Shortly afterward a summons from the emperor arrived at Yoshitomo's mansion, ordering him to seek out and execute all his younger siblings, especially Tametomo, whose martial prowess was deemed the greatest threat to the imperial house. The shrewd Tametomo had already escaped into exile. But his five brothers were captured and taken to Funaoka Hill, just north of the capital, where they ended their lives as true warriors.

The ordeal was not yet over. The Minato were a prolific breed, and no sooner had Yoshitomo heard the dreadful news than he received another imperial summons, reminding him that he had yet more brothers, who, though only infants, should also be put to death. All four of them, the eldest no older than thirteen years, were likewise taken to Funaoka Hill, where, with a show of courage befitting mature warriors, they ended their lives. Their attendants, who had reared the boys from infancy, all committed ritual suicide. Unable to bear the unbearable, their mother, Tameyoshi's wife, filled the wide sleeves of her kimono with stones and threw herself into the Katsura River.

Never before in the long history of the Japanese realm had an imperial dispute led to such gratuitous bloodshed. It had been a senseless act, the brainchild of a sycophant, which could have been averted by a forgiving emperor had he but shown the faintest glimmer of humanity. For Taira Kiyomori it became the stepping stone toward his coveted ascendancy. For Minamoto Yoshitomo it was a private tragedy that put to naught his rise in the world, and a public defeat that cast a long dark shadow over all the Minamoto victories that would follow. Had the sentiments of his great-grandfather, Yoshiie, been those of resentment and indignation, those of Yoshitomo and his descendants were those of a black and seething hatred—a desire beyond death to wipe from the face of the earth the clan whose members had conspired in the decline, the impoverishment, and the humiliation of the once so glorious Minamoto.

# A New Status Quo

Whatever the feelings between the two rival clans, the imperial succession dispute had thrust both into the forefront of national politics. For centuries the clans had dutifully served the imperial court—they still did, but a profound change had taken place nevertheless.

Thus far, the military clans had had no direct say or leverage over national policy; all they had to do was to uphold the authority of the court by suppressing local rebellions that threatened to undermine it. In the process, the court had come to rely increasingly on the Minamoto and the Taira, but on the whole, it had usually had a free hand in the nomination of the *tsuitōshi*. The Hōgen Insurrection had dramatically changed all this. Now the court itself was the source of unrest, and now the decision as to who was to suppress whom lay not with the court and its Military Council, but with the military chieftains themselves. It was a profound change, as it now made the court dependent upon the whims and wiles of the military leaders. For more than two centuries the leaders of the military clans had reverently submitted

## Chūjō Hyōgo no Kami Nagahide

to the will of the imperial court, in awe as they were of its grandeur and prestige. The unseemly and mundane power struggle between the two imperial rivals and their own indispensable role in its quelling, had taught the military, as nothing else could have taught them, that it was they who really held the strings by which the puppets at court played their insignificant roles. Their full insinuation into the corridors of power, first announced by that sinister and ominous performance at the evening banquet by Taira Tadamori, was now an incontrovertible fact. From now on they played an integral part in the complex and intricate machinations of the power brokers at court. No daughter of noble birth could reach a marriageable age without her parents at least considering a member of the military, however much she might protest. No nobleman could aspire to a position at court without the backing of at least one of the military clans, however much he might detest their boorish and bloody ways. No move, then, of any political significance could be made without taking into serious consideration its repercussions on the fragile balance of power between the Minamoto and the Taira.

In the wake of the Hōgen Insurrection, the presence of the chieftains of the military clans on the national stage had become so prominent that even the once so powerful Fujiwara were forced to directly include the leaders of the military in their political schemes. And it was one of their members, Fu-

Taira Tadamori captures a wandering oil thief on behalf of Emperor Shirakawa

# Famous Samurai: The Two Courts Period

jiwara Nobuyori, the colonel of the Gate Guards of the Right, who, on a dark and windswept autumn evening, called at the mansion of the Active Chief of the Left Division of the Horse Bureau, the general who had quelled the Hōgen Insurrection, Minamoto Yoshitomo. It was an evening in keeping with the sentiments that led the colonel to the solitary mansion of this prematurely old and tragic figure, for Nobuyori had evil designs.

The suppression of the Hōgen Insurrection had done little to reduce the conspiracies at court. There were still factions that contended for supremacy and sought to achieve their aims by rallying behind imperial rivals. In the latest imperial dispute there were two such rivals: the retired emperor Go-Shirakawa and the newly crowned emperor, his son, Nijō. Inevitably, there were also two factions. The one to which Nobuyori belonged had taken the side of Nijō; the other was in collusion with Go-Shirakawa. They were led

The fellow conspirators Fujiwara Nobuyori and Minamoto Yoshitomo

by the Counselor of State, Fujiwara Michinori, who had taken the tonsure and assumed the name of Shinzei.

Shinzei was a formidable opponent. He was a financial wizard, who had restored the faltering finances of the court by reviving the trade with China. This had brought him into contact with Taira Kiyomori, and soon there had sprung up between the two intellects a deep friendship. That friendship was built on both men's awareness that each could benefit from the other: Shinzei saw in Kiyomori a powerful military ally; Kiyomori simply considered all connections with the court a benefit. The chief reason for Nobuyori's dislike of Shinzei was that the latter had managed to thwart Nobuyori's promotion to that of Great Commander of the Imperial Bodyguards. Only recently Nobuyori had been nominated for the post, and even though the emperor had made it clear that he favored Nobuyori, Shinzei had dissuaded Go-Shirakawa from doing so.

Yoshitomo had not been Nobuyori's first choice. Through and through opportunist that he was, Nobuyori had naturally gravitated toward the glamor of the Taira. In order to strengthen his ties with them, he had already considered having his son marry one of Kiyomori's daughters, but had given up on the idea as the Taira were currently in favor at court and they were unlikely to conspire in any schemes that would threaten its, and their, position. Yoshitomo, he knew, would be a far more pliable candidate. Did not everyone know of the humiliations the chieftain had been made to endure at the hand of the Taira? But few, even not Yoshitomo, knew that the man who had urged the emperor not to show any leniency toward his father and his many brothers was none other than Shinzei. And thus Nobuyori revealed to Yoshitomo the true role the lay monk had played in the retributions following the Hōgen Insurrection. It must have been with an inward smile that he observed the effect of his words on the warrior, and that he hastened to assure Yoshitomo that if he, Nobuyori, were to be in Shinzei's position the emperor would surely be favorably inclined if Yoshitomo were to ask for a return of his estates and promotion in rank. It did not take Yoshitomo long to decide on whose side he was willing to fight, and that same night the two men drew up their first plans on how rid themselves of the hated Shinzei and his ally Kiyomori.

Famous Samurai: The Two Courts Period

## The Heiji Insurrection

Not long after the conspirator's nightly rendezvous, on December 4, 1159, the first year of Heiji, Kiyomori and his family left the capital for Kumano, on the southern border of Yamato province. The statesman had once made a vow that he would make a pilgrimage to the famous shrine at Kumano, but recent events had kept him from doing so.

This was the chance Nobuyori and Yoshitomo had been waiting for. Five days after Kiyomori had departed from his official residence at Rokuhara, Yoshitomo and an army of some five hundred warriors marched on the Sanjō palace, the residence of the retired emperor Go-Shirakawa, whom they seized and locked up in the palace library. Then they took out their revenge on the hated Taira. The *Heiji monogatari*, the only full account of this gruesome episode in the closing decades of the Heian period, describes the ruthlessness with which the coup was executed:

> While warriors secured the gates, fire was set at various places. Furious flames filled the sky and violent winds swept up clouds of smoke. Nobles, courtiers, down to the court-ladies, were all shot or cut down in the assumption that they, too, might be members of Shinzei's household. When they rushed out to escape the fire, they were met by arrows, and when they returned to escape the arrows they were met by flames. Others, who feared the arrows and sought to escape the flames, even threw themselves into the wells in great numbers, so that, before long, those at the bottom were drowned, those in the middle crushed, and those at the top burned by the searing flames.

That same night they attacked Shinzei's residence in similar fashion. But the lay monk himself was nowhere to be found. He had fled with four of his attendants to Tawara, a mountainous region southeast of Uji. There they dug a pit with a small exhaust to breathe through. On their return to the capital, however, one of the attendants was captured by Yoshitomo's men and forced to lead them to his master's hideout. When they found him, Shinzei was still alive, but they beheaded him nevertheless and took his head to the capital.

### Chūjō Hyōgo no Kami Nagahide

The rebels set fire to the Sanjō palace

Meanwhile all of his twelve sons had been rounded up and thrown into prison awaiting banishment into exile. The last glimpse they got of their father was through the bars of their prison cells, for his head had been attached to the prison gate for all to see. When all this was done the conspirators congratulated each other on their easy victory, appointing themselves to the high offices they had coveted. Nobuyori was made Great Commander of the Imperial Bodyguards, and Yoshitomo governor of Harima.

At this juncture Yoshitomo's eldest son, Yoshihira, arrived with fresh troops from Kamakura. He reminded the ringleaders that their most dangerous enemy was still alive. Being an experienced commander, Yoshihira proposed leading an advance party to Abeno, a plain south of Osaka, in order to await and intercept Kiyomori on his return from his pilgrimage. But the idea was rejected by Nobuyori, who thought it far more prudent to wait until Kiyomori had returned to his residence at Rokuhara and surprise him there. Thus it was that the ignorance of a courtier again won out over the experience of a warrior and that the chance of victory had been lost through complacency.

# Famous Samurai: The Two Courts Period

Emperor Nijō makes his escape

By then, Kiyomori, who was still on his way to the Kumano shrine, had got wind of the coup. On the day following the attack on the Sanjō Palace, a messenger from Rokuhara had caught up with him at the post station of Kiribe, on route to Kumano. Taking in what had happened, he immediately decided to abandon the pilgrimage and return to the capital. Given the purpose of their journey, all of them were wearing the traditional pilgrim garb, and it was only with the help of a related local chieftain, Taira Iesada, that he was able to arm his men. That night, without hindrance from Yoshitomo's men, they arrived at the Rokuhara. No sooner had they done so, than Kiyomori sent a messenger bearing a conciliatory letter to the conspirators. By thus winning time, he and his followers were able to reinforce their position at his Rokuhara mansion in preparation for a standoff. Nothing, however, happened, and for the next few days he and his men waited with bated breath, "milling about at Rokuhara, expecting an attack from the palace, while at the palace the warriors were milling about, expecting an attack from Rokuhara."

Go-Shirakawa had already managed to make his escape to a monastery on the northwestern edge of the capital. His son, too, was uncomfortable with the vulnerable position into which he had been placed by the coup. The continuous nocturnal drinking parties at the palace, presided over by an intoxicated Nobuyori, inspired little confidence in his political skills, and Nijō sensed that Kiyomori's might well be the winning faction. During one of the parties, on the evening of December 25, he made up his mind. Disguising himself as a lady-in-waiting, he slipped out of the palace unnoticed, arriving that same evening at the headquarters of his father's faction.

# A Tactical Blunder

The effect of Nijō's defection to Kiyomori's camp was instant. Many courtiers who had thus far gone along with the coup to save their own skins now thought it prudent to reconsider their positions and rallied around the emperor. They were followed by a great number of warriors, thus restoring the great imbalance in troop numbers that had existed between the two camps, and that night Kiyomori ordered his commanders to launch a full-scale attack against the imperial palace at dawn.

At the palace, learning of the emperor's defection, Yoshitomo remained undaunted. He ordered his eldest son, Yoshihira, to make a roll-call of the troops who had remained loyal and prepare to defend the imperial palace, with or without its resident. They concentrated their forces at the Yōmei, Taiken, and Ikuhō gates, all gates in the eastern walls of the greater imperial palace enclosure, from where they expected the Taira assault. Nobuyori, too, made ready for battle, but his appearance and demeanor instilled little confidence in the Kantō warriors. Their fears were confirmed the next morning, when Kiyomori marched on the palace at the head of a force of three thousand troops and Nobuyori and his men, who had taken up positions at the Taiken gate, fell back before a fierce assault that was led by Kiyomori's son, Shigemori. Encouraged by Nobuyori's flight, the Taira forces managed to penetrate as far as the imperial palace compound, where they were confronted by Yoshihira and some seventeen warriors, and driven out.

## Famous Samurai: The Two Courts Period

Had Yoshitomo at this juncture ordered his men to regroup and secure the Taiken gate, he might have saved the day. Instead, he ordered his men to give chase. Dutifully, they did so, all the way to Rokuhara. It was a tactical blunder. No sooner had the Minamoto forces crossed the Kamo River, than the government forces took repossession of the imperial palace.

The attack on Rokuhara, too, came to naught. When Yoshitomo eventually ordered his men to withdraw there was no safe place to retreat to. They set off eastward, across the mountains east of the capital, toward the western shore of Lake Biwa. From there Yoshitomo hoped to embark by boat, and cross the lake toward Hikone and the Fuwa barrier. Situated at the point where the Ibuki and Yōrō mountains converged, the Fuwa barrier formed the gateway between eastern and western Japan, and Yoshitomo knew that, once they had passed the Fuwa barrier, they would be relatively safe from persecution. But already during the first leg of their journey they ran into serious trouble when, while crossing the Ryūge pass, they came under attack from a large force of *sōhei* from the Enryaku monastery, which was allied to the retired emperor Go-Shirakawa. Many of Yoshitomo's men, including his second son, Tomonaga, were wounded in the attack, but most of them eventually managed to drive their way through and reach the shore of Lake Biwa. As the day drew on, a fierce storm struck up from the east and they could not find any fishermen willing to ferry them across. Abandoning his initial plan, Yoshitomo now proceeded southward, following the lake's shores, through Ōtsu and Seta, in the hope of thus reaching the Fuwa barrier. Before he did so, he ordered most of his commanders to take their men and return to their various provinces. Reluctantly they complied, and it was only after most of them had returned to the safety of their strongholds that they learned of the tragic fate of their leader and his three valiant sons.

## Through the Snow

Following their departure from Ōtsu, Yoshitomo and his sons had hurried on, eastward, hoping to make it to the barrier before dark. But they had made little headway. It was in the dead of winter, a cold wind was blowing from the east, and Tomonaga's wound made it impossible for them to spur on their horses. Knowing that the barrier would by now be heavily guarded, and fearing that they might be detected, they had left the Tōkaidō shortly before they had reached the Fuwa barrier, keeping it on their left hand side until they had reached the town of Ibuki. From there they had skirted the southern slopes of mount Ibuki in order to bypass the Fuwa barrier. By then darkness had set in, and snow was falling thick and fast on the mountain's exposed slopes, making it hard to tell where they were going. They had plodded on, and when their horses were exhausted and no longer able to carry the burden, donned their heavy armor to proceed on foot through the deep snow. To travel light, they had even abandoned the precious family heirloom.

It was during this part of the journey that Yoshitomo's third son, Yoritomo, began to trail behind more and more, until, by the time they had crossed into Mino province, they had lost all sight of him. Finally, after a

## Famous Samurai: The Two Courts Period

cold and stormy night, they had reached the hamlet of Aohaka, where they found shelter at the home of a local ally.

Yet their situation was getting more desperate with the moment. Already Yoshitomo had lost his third son in the snow, and now he had to watch as Tomonaga was deteriorating before his eyes. The wound he had incurred during the attack of the *sōhei* of Mount Hiei had ruptured during the journey. He had lost so much blood that was unable to go on. Knowing what fate would await him on capture, he pleaded with his father to administer the coup de grace and relieve him from his misery. Blinded by tears the desperate father obliged. Then he instructed his oldest son, Yoshihira, to take the road northward, to the Hokuriku region, in order to raise troops with the help of local allies and continue the struggle with the Taira. He himself set out toward the Kantō in the company of his last four retainers, a broken man, distraught and disoriented by grief.

The Ibuki Mountains, looming large against a cold evening sky

Reaching the province of Owari, Yoshitomo and his men found refuge at the house of Osada Tadamune, the father-in-law of his most loyal retainer, Kamada Masakiyo. It was his last and most fateful error. Tadamune, too, had gone over to the camp of Kiyomori. He offered Yoshitomo a hot bath to recover from the cold. The warrior gratefully accepted the offer, and left Masakiyo to guard the entrance. Thus it was, naked and defenseless, that the Minamoto chieftain was treacherously slain. Hearing the commotion, his vassal rushed in after him, but it was too late. He, too, was murdered by his hosts, comforting his master as he fell: "Masakiyo joins you my lord."

## Local Repercussions

The combined effect of the Hōgen and Heiji Insurrections constituted a devastating blow to the Minamoto clan, as well as their many vassal clans. Many of the warrior commanders who had been with Yoshitomi when he ejected the rebels from the Shirakawa palace had joined him in the Heiji Insurrection. On the roll-call of defensive forces Yoshitomo had ordered his son to make had been some of his most trusted vassal chieftains, men such as Chiba Hirotsune, and Ōgo Shigetoshi, a warrior from the province of Kōzuke. Yet from all his vassals who had come down from the Kantō, it was again those from the province of Musashi who were most numerous. Many of them belonged to one of the houses of the Musashi Nanadō.

The warriors of the house of Narita, too, had joined Yoshitomo in battle. During the Hōgen Insurrection, when they were still fighting on the side of the imperial court, they had fought alongside the troops of their new governor, Chūjō Tsunemitsu, whose forces were led by his fifth and sixth son, Shingo and Shinroku. First among the warriors of the Narita clan to be mentioned by the chroniclers of the *Hōgen monogatari* was Narita Sukehiro. Respectful of a man's pedigree, they had referred to him as Narita no Tarō, that is, the firstborn of Narita Suketaka, the founder of the Narita clan. He was followed by his brother Yukitaka, alias Beppu Jirō, the second son of Suketaka, whose estate lay northwest of Kumagaya. Next in line was Takanaga, alias Nara Saburō, the third son of Suketaka, whose estate lay north of Ku-

# Famous Samurai: The Two Courts Period

magaya. He was followed by Sukezane, alias Tamai Shirō, the fourth son of Suketaka, whose estate lay west of Kumagaya. During the Heiji Insurrection they had continued to fight alongside Yoshitomo's forces, although this time directly under his own command, as the governor had prudently withdrawn. All had survived the skirmishes unscathed and had grudgingly complied with Yoshitomo's orders to return home after they had crossed the Ryūge pass to Ōtsu. They made it past the Fuwa barrier in time, only learning of the tragic fate of their leader on their return home.

It had been an ignominious end, unworthy of a great warrior. To add insult to injury, Yoshitomo's head had been sent to the capital to be exposed to the public as that of an ordinary rebel. Shortly after this sad news, it was followed by that of Yoshihira's death. Going against his father's wishes, he had smuggled himself back into the capital—what for it was hard to fathom, perhaps to see his mistress or maybe to avenge his father by assassinating Kiyomori. Like so many others he was caught and beheaded.

Not, however, before he had been interrogated by a somewhat puzzled Kiyomori. How, the latter had asked, could a man who had conquered a hundred warriors with seventeen handpicked men be caught so easily? The answer had unsettled the interrogator. Yoshihira calmly observed that it was his fate to die, as his luck had run out. Soon, he warned Kiyomori, his luck would also run out. Then he, too, would have to come to terms with the retribution fate had in store for him.

The ultimate repercussions of this dreadful news came soon afterward. All the Kantō chieftains embroiled in the plot were relieved of their posts with immediate effect, and all their ranks and titles taken away. Though of no material value, these were status symbols of great importance to the self-esteem of the medieval warrior. The greatest shock to their sense of pride was that most of the lands for which they had fought so hard were taken away from them. They were confiscated by the state and awarded to the few Kantō warriors who had chosen the side of the Taira.

Amid all these bad tidings and setbacks there had been one ray of light for the Kantō warriors who had remained loyal to the Minamoto. The thirteen-year-old Yoritomo, whom Yoshitomo had given up as lost, had survived the ordeal on the slopes of Mount Ibuki in spite of his tender age. Having

*Opposite page*: Minamoto Yoshitomo is treacherously murdered by Tadamune and his henchmen lost sight of his father and brothers on that fateful journey, he had stubbornly plodded on through the deep snow until he had stumbled on a small village called Kodaira. He had lost his bearing and had ended up on the western side of the mountain, still within the grasp of Kiyomori's henchmen. Unable to go on, he had gone into hiding in the Asai district, where he was taken in by an old nun. When the snow had melted he had set out to find his father. Having safely passed the barrier, he covered much of the journey through Mino by water in the small boat of a cormorant fisher. But having reached the province of Owari, he was caught and taken to Okazaki, to the headquarters of the province's governor, Taira Yorimori. The future seemed bleak for the young warrior for Yorimori was Kiyomori's stepbrother.

Yorimori was also the son of Tadamori's second wife, Ike no Zen'ni, who lived at her son's mansion. The young orphan reminded her of a child she had once lost, and when the boy was sent to Rokuhara to be executed, she pleaded with her stepson to spare the young boy's life. Her tears were not without effect. Somewhere in that dark mind, there must have been a spark of humanity, for Kiyomori obliged by commuting Yoritomo's life-sentence to one of exile. This rare act of benevolence did not fit well in the long train of gruesome events he had set in motion. By killing his own uncle in the Kamo riverbed, he had brought down over the heads of his clan-members the eternal wrath of the Minamoto. Such unbridled hatred could not be undone with one mere act of benevolence, and thus, the man who had risen to the fore with such unscrupulous ruthlessness sealed his fate with the only act of benevolence he ever allowed himself.

Yoritomo was sent to Izu, where he was placed in the care of a court official by the name of Hōjō Tokimasa. The young boy spent a free enough youth on and around the grounds of Tokimasa's manor, and soon impressed his guardian with his sharp intelligence and incisive actions. He also impressed Tokimasa's daughter, whom he married shortly after he had reached manhood at the age of sixteen.

Yet Yoritomo's childhood was not one free of cares. Ever since he had last beheld his father and his brothers, fading out of sight in the driving blizzards on the slopes of Mount Ibuki, their tragic fate—a fate to which he, too, should have been condemned—had been foremost in his mind. He knew

## Chūjō Hyōgo no Kami Nagahide

there was only one way to redress the many wrongs that had been done to them and to those who had gone before them: to crush the Taira and wipe them from the face of the earth.

It was not long, then after his arrival at Hōjō Tokimasa's manor that the young warrior was entertaining secret communications with a large number of the Kantō chieftains who had sided with his father during the Hōgen and Heiji Insurrections and remained loyal to the Minamoto cause. They deeply empathized with the sad loss of the orphan, but more importantly, they understood the sentiments that drove the young warrior on better than anybody else. Theirs, after all, was a shared destiny, equally sealed in the blood of their men and powered by the same sense of pride. To them Yoritomo's survival and his ambition to redress all the injustices that had been done to his clan held out new hopes—hopes for the long-awaited restoration of the fortunes of the Minamoto and their own.

The time, however, was not yet ripe. Twenty more years they had to wait. They did so patiently and unfalteringly, until the young orphan had grown into an adult warrior and raised the banner of revolt. His first act was to attack the mansion of the acting governor of Izu, Yamaki Kanetaka.

Yoritomo and his men attack the mansion of Yamaki Kanetaka

## Famous Samurai: The Two Courts Period

Yoritomo and his men hide in the hollow of a tree to avoid capture

His first serious battle, fought on the slopes of Mount Ishibashi, not far from the village to which he had been exiled, he lost. It was almost the end of him. He was utterly routed, and only managed to escape capture with a handful of his retainers by hiding in a rotten hollow of a large Japanese cypress. From there they had fled across the water, to the Bōsō Peninsula. And it had been from there, and with the help of local chieftains that he had gone on to achieve his first victory over the Taira. The struggle between the Minamoto and the Taira, know as the Gempei War, was a long and arduous one. It was fought out between 1180 and 1185 in numerous battles at even so numerous venues. But eventually it led to Yoritomo's victory in the sea-battle at Dannoura—a victory all the more remarkable, as it were the Taira, from the Bay of Ise, who were used to fighting at sea.

## The Kantō Chieftains

When Yoritomo rose in revolt, all of the clans of the Musashi Nanadō who had fought with him and his father during the Hōgen and Heiji disturbances rallied under his banner: the Hirayama, the Kodama, the Murayama, the Inomata, and, not to forget, the many descendants of the Yokoyamadō: the Narita, the Beppu, the Nara, and the Tamai. Narita Sukehiro meanwhile had handed over the reigns of his clan to his son Suketsuna, who fought alongside Yoritomo in most of the battles of the Gempei war, and was with him when he finally crushed the Taira at the battle of Dannoura. Suketsuna's moment of glory came in the summer of 1190, when he and some three hundred Kantō warriors accompanied Minamoto Yoritomo when he entered the capital in panoply and was appointed commander of the Imperial Left Guard. Two years later Suketsuna was again present when, on , 1192, at the new headquarters of the Bakufu in Kamakura, Yoritomo was officially appointed "Barbarian subduing Generalissimo," or Sei-i Tai-Shōgun, an appointment only made possible by the demise of Emperor Go-Shirakawa, who had resisted the appointment up until his dying day.

As in all feudal societies, Yoritomo's successes percolated down through the ranks of his vassals, especially those who had remained loyal to him and his ancestors through the long and difficult years of the Taira ascendancy. Sukehiro's son, Suketsuna, as well as his grandson, Moritsuna, had played a decisive role in the battle of Ichinotani, in which the forces of Yoritomo's brother Yoshitsune dealt a resounding blow to the Taira forces. Upon the

The numerous Kantō clans rally under the Minamoto banner

## Famous Samurai: The Two Courts Period

founding of the Kamakura Bakufu they were made *gokenin*, direct retainers of the shogun. On Suketsuna's death at the turn of the twelfth century, his estate was inherited by Moritsuna, but Moritsuna failed to sustain his father's success. The reason for that failure had little to do with his qualities, but everything with the rivalry that had sprung up between the new Kamakura Bakufu and the ancient imperial court.

Following his victory over the Taira at Dannoura, Yoritomo had been left with one great problem: what to do with the imperial court? In a society that viewed the emperor as divine, it was unthinkable to abolish the imperial house, yet something had to be done to curtail the political influence of the court. Go-Shirakawa's death had temporarily removed such interference, but his grandson, Go-Toba soon learned that cloister government was the tool by which he might reclaim political influence. In 1198, still only eighteen years old, and without consulting the Bakufu, he abdicated in favor of his son and took the tonsure. This put Yoritomo in a difficult position. He had depended on the infant emperor for his appointment as shogun, but he died before he was able to overcome his reluctance to intervene. Capitalizing on the power struggle that ensued within the Bakufu, Go-Toba now began to reinforce his position by recruiting powerful *gokenin* from Japan's eastern and

The Battle of Dannoura, the Minamoto's final victory over the Taira

western provinces as imperial guards. It was a stroke of genius, for in doing so, he formed the core of an army that could challenge the authority of the Bakufu. He could furthermore count on the support of the Enryaku and Kō-fuku monasteries, the bastions of power of the Tendai and Hossō sects. Always at loggerheads with each other, both sects had been repeatedly suppressed by the warrior chieftains and their religious leaders were more than willing to contribute their vast armies of *sōhei* to the lofty cause of imperial restoration by their fellow monk.

It so happened that one of the Kantō chieftains who had been recruited to serve on the imperial guard was Narita Moritsuna. Already his older brother, Yoshisuke, had done his tour of duty, and not long after he had succeeded his father it was Moritsuna's turn to leave his estate in the care of his brothers and take up residence in the capital. He did so reluctantly. Indeed, it is unlikely that he would have chosen to fight against the very institution that had brought such prosperity to his family, had it not been for the vicious power struggle that broke out within the Bakufu on Yoritomo's death.

The power struggle centered around his eldest son and successor, Yoriie, a young man of limited abilities. In physical prowess, the son outshone his father, but Yoriie had a wild and unruly nature, and where it came to the conducting of day-to-day affairs he was wholly lacking. For some time the administrative burden was carried by a council composed of the chieftains of the warrior clans, but it did not take long before they began to quarrel among each other. Several contenders came to the fore, and it was a member of the Hōjō, the shrewd and unassuming Tokimasa, who eventually emerged as the new Bakufu regent by crushing his rivals and assuming the role of *shikken*, or regent to the infant shogun.

The change of leadership left many eastern chieftains dissatisfied. Important posts had been left vacant, and men who had enjoyed high rank under Yoritomo were neglected or simply ignored by the Hōjō. Then, on June 5, 1221, seeking to capitalize on the discontent among the Bakufu ranks, Go-Toba issued an edict in which he solemnly denounced the then *shikken*, Tokimasa's son Yasutoki, as an outlaw.

Whatever reasons Moritsuna may have had to choose the side of Go-Toba, his was not a prudent move, as the majority of the Kantō warrior clans remained loyal to the Bakufu. They vastly outnumbered the imperial troops, whose ranks were made up of undisciplined and inexperienced soldiers. Exactly one month later, on July 5, Go-Toba was forced to withdraw his edict and again submit to Tokimasa's rule.

Thus the Jōkyū Rebellion, so named after the era in which it occurred, came to an ignominious end. For Go-Toba it merely meant that his court once more had to kowtow to the wishes of the Bakufu. For those who had fought for his cause there were only two ways to escape persecution, death or exile. It was in death that Moritsuna had found his exit. He had fallen on July 4, when the remnants of the imperial troops made a last valiant stand on the western banks of the Uji River. For some hours they managed to withstand the onslaught, but eventually they too were scattered before Yasutoki's superior forces.

# The Chūjō Clan

Moritsuna and his brothers were the only members of the Narita clan to have fought with the imperial troops, and in the clamp-down that followed the chieftains of the Beppu, Nara, and Tamai, were able to hold on to their possessions. Moritsuna had no heirs and his lands were inherited by his cousin Ienaga, but not under the clan name of Narita. Well before the young Ienaga had come of age his father had become disillusioned with warrior life and laid aside his armor to enter a monastery. Ienaga had been adopted by Hatta Tomoie, a prominent Minamoto vassal. It was an arrangement typical of a feudal society in which the ever looming threat of covetous neighbors made the continuation of the family line by necessity subservient to that of the martial tradition.

For the young Ienaga adoption brought wealth and prestige. Hatta Tomoie was the constable of Hitachi province and a prosperous chieftain. He hailed from Shimotsuke, and was the scion of the Utsunomiya, a powerful clan, which descended from the even more powerful Fujiwara, and a clan whose many strands had spread as far south as Kyushu and as far north as Dewa province. Like Ienaga's ancestors, the Utsunomiya had also been close vassals of the Minamoto, and like them, they, too, had felt the wrath of the Taira in the wake of the Heiji Insurrection. The ties between the two clans had become particularly close at the time of Tomoie and Yoritomo, who had spent their childhoods together in exile and were like brothers to each other. Some even believed that they were exactly that, as Tomoie's mother, Samugawani, had at a young age served in the Minamoto household as Yoritomo's wet nurse and rumors had it that Yoshitomo had taken a particular liking to her. Tomoie had played an important role in the Gempei war and his rewards were commensurate. He was given the large estate of Tsukuba in the province of Hitachi and had been appointed constable of the province in 1185. Shortly after his appointment he had begun on the construction of a large castle, one of the first of its kind, which was completed in 1192 and named Oda, after the small hamlet situated on his estate. As was the custom, Tomoie, too, took on the name of the locality in which it had settled, thus becoming the distant ancestor of Oda Haruhisa, the warlord under whose

Only part of the ramparts and moats Oda castle have survived

## Famous Samurai: The Two Courts Period

rule the castle became the shelter of the great strategist of the Loyalist campaign, Kitabatake Chikafusa.

Ienaga did not succeed Tomoie as leader of the Oda clan, Having many stepbrothers, he was required to make a name for himself on his own strength. He did so with remarkable fervor. Returning to Musashi and the estate he had inherited from his father, he built a large mansion on the outskirts of Kumagaya. Close by, he erected the Jōkō-in, a monastery dedicated to the memory of his ancestors and patronized by the Chūjō clan ever since. Known for his accomplishments in both military and civil affairs, he quickly rose within the Bakufu ranks, At the end of the 1220s, he reached the highest echelons of the Bakufu hierarchy when he became a member of the Hyōjōshū, the Board of Councilors. This organ, founded by in 1225 by Hōjō Yasutoki was the Bakufu's highest decision-making organ of government. In his new position Ienaga played an important role in the compilation of the

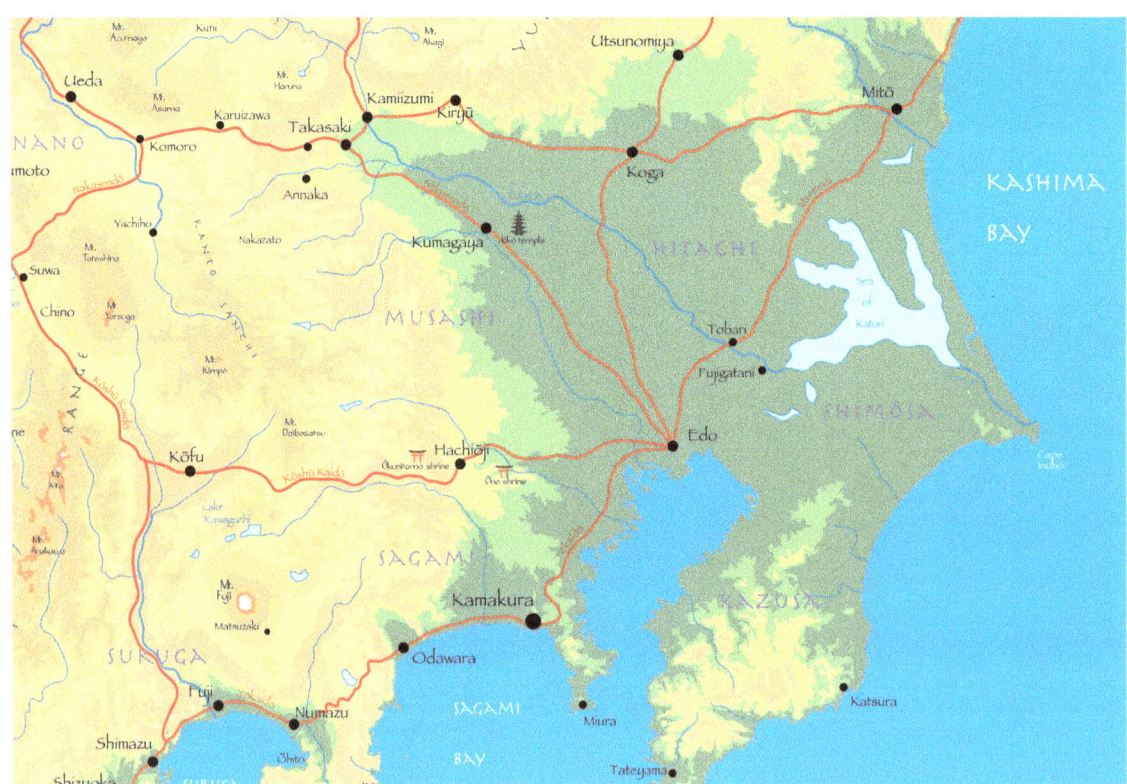

# Chūjō Hyōgo no Kami Nagahide

Kumagaya's Jōkō-in, the monastery founded by Chūjō Ienaga

*Goseibai shikimoku*. This feudal piece of legislation, promulgated in 1232, served to regulate the conduct of the Bakufu's many vassals. It was the first warrior code of its kind, and served as a blueprint for all future warrior codes. Ienaga's achievements did not go down in history under the name of Oda, nor that of Narita, for the name the Bakufu official assumed after he returned to Kumagaya was that of Chūjō, and it was under that name that his descendants made their mark on events over the next three centuries.

It is not clear what made Ienaga decide to adopt the name of Chūjō; he was, after all, a Narita. Was it simply because the land on which he had built his new residence happened to carry the name of Chūjō? Was it the shame brought on the name of Narita when his uncle had chosen to fight on the side of the imperial troops during the Jōkyū disturbance? Or was it his wish to preserve the memory of Chūjō Tsunemitsu, the governor of Musashi in whose name his ancestors had fought so bravely during the Heiji

Insurrection? It had been to his memory, after all, that he had dedicated the temple he had built on the grounds of his estate. If so, it was also a strategic choice, as Tsunemitsu was, like Ienaga's adoptive family the Utsunomiya, of Fujiwara descent. Perhaps it was a combination of all these factors, for the full name he assumed on his return to Musashi was Chūjō Tōji Ienaga, the middle name—a Chinese reading of the characters connoting "successor to the Fuji(wara),"—clearly denoting his proud link to the powerful clan of Heian regents.

In doing so, Ienaga laid the foundations for a clan that was to survive well into the sixteenth century. For it was in 1561 that one of Ienaga's distant descendants, a certain Chūjō Tsunetaka, was defeated by Japan's first great unifier, Oda Nobunaga. Deprived of his castle and estate, Tsunetaka retired to a small mansion where, on November 4, 1573, he died penniless and without leaving any heirs. During the four centuries of its existence the Chūjō clan was to know many moments of glory, and it was such a period that coincided with the life of the second great swordsman of the Two Courts period, Chūjō Hyōgo no Kami Nagahide.

# Koromo Castle

Chūjō Nagahide was born many hundreds of miles from the region where the proud history of his clan began. It had been during the middle of the thirteenth century, that one of Ienaga's descendants, a certain Chūjō Yorihira, had been appointed as constable of Owari province. He had settled in Takahashi, a district just over the border with Mikawa, along the Yahagi River.

Yorihira had three sons, each of whom made it into important position within the Bakufu hierarchy. His eldest son, Nagamune, became governor of Izu. His second son, Kagenaga, became governor of Dewa, a post that had for several generations belonged to the Chūjō. His youngest son, Hidenaga, stayed at home to manage and protect the family estate. Of the three, Kagenaga proved the most talented, and where his brothers were content with the roles they had been given, Kagenaga's ambitious nature caused him to steadily rise among the Bakufu ranks, until, in 1309, he followed in his an-

## Chūjō Hyōgo no Kami Nagahide

cestor's footsteps by becoming a member of the Board of Councilors. It was Kagenaga, therefore, and not Nagamune, who succeeded his father when the latter retired into a Buddhist monastery. Though he spent much of his time in Kamakura, Kagenaga held on to his family's estate in Mikawa, where, at the turn of the thirteenth century, he began on the construction of a modest castle, half a mile west of the Yahagi River.

In 1333, in spite of the prosperity their clan had known under rule of the Kamakura Bakufu, the brothers, like so many other former Kantō clans, joined the side of Go-Daigo and helped bring about the Kenmu Restoration. Being lieged to the Ashikaga house, they had not marched on Kamakura with Nitta Yoshisada, but had joined Ashikaga Takauji on his drive westward to seize the capital for the Loyalists. Following Takauji's revolt they had remained loyal to their overlord, and in the long contest between the two rival courts over the next five decades, they had frequently clashed with the Loy-

# Famous Samurai: The Two Courts Period

alist forces. It was in one of those battles, fought close to home on the banks of the Yahagi River, that Kagenaga was gravely wounded. He eventually recovered, but his injuries left him so severely disabled that he was unable to fight ever again. Unable to continue his heavy burden of responsibilities, he decided to follow in the footsteps of his father, assuming the Buddhist name of Kagekiyo and spending the rest of his days in quietude on his Takahashi estate. By this time he had one infant son, Nagahide. The boy had been born shortly after the Kenmu Restoration, and since he was only a few years old and Nagamune far away in Dewa, the reigns of power within the Chūjō clan were passed on to the youngest of the three brothers, Hidenaga.

Hidenaga became a worthy regent. Frugal, conscientious, and always energetic, he proved a very effective chieftain and managed the financial affairs of his family's estate with the same thoroughness with which he led the men under his command. His talents were soon recognized by the newly established Muromachi Bakufu, which, within only years after Hidenaga had taken

The Chōkō temple, founded by Chūjō Hidenaga

## Chūjō Hyōgo no Kami Nagahide

The Sanage shrine, built at the southern foot of Mount Sanage

the place of his brother, appointed him as constable of Owari, thus causing the office to be held by three members of the Chūjō clan in succession.

Toward the middle of the fourteenth century, at the height of his career, Hidenaga was appointed as the governor of Bizen. At home he continued the various projects his brother had begun, completing the construction of the family castle, which he named Koromo, after the hamlet on whose outskirts it arose. Around roughly the same time, he began work on the construction of a large temple, situated on the western bank of the Yahagi River. On its completion a few years later, he named it the Chōkō temple, *chō* being the Chinese reading of the second character of his own given name. Hidenaga was also a great patron of Shinto tradition, contributing large tracts of land to the local shrine of Sanage, situated at the foot of the eponymous mountain, a few miles north of Koromo. It is at the Sanage shrine that many of the Chūjō family records have been preserved to this very day.

# Famous Samurai: The Two Courts Period

## Bunbu Ryōdō

The Chūjō brothers belonged to that class of aristocratic warriors equally at home in the realm of civil and martial accomplishments. The belief in the dictum of *bunbu ryōdō*, the dual way of learning and fighting already practiced by Ono Takamura, the poet-scholar who had been exiled to Oki island after he had withdrawn from the imperial mission to China. It had been turned into an art by the members of the Yokoyamadō—an art that, through Ienaga, had been passed down the lines of the Chūjō clan. The three Chūjō brothers, too, spent a lot of time in the pursuit of knowledge and in the development and transmission of the style of fencing that had been practiced by their ancestors—a style of fencing that had seen all of them safely through the many conflicts of the preceding centuries: the Hōgen and Heiji insurrections, the many campaigns of the Gempei war and the countless battles in the run-up to and the aftermath of the Kenmu Restoration.

According to the family records of the Chūjō clan, their particular style of fencing went right back to none other than Ono Takamura. It was true that in Takamura's time the bow had taken precedence over the sword, and it had been chiefly for his archery and horsemanship that the towering Heian nobleman had impressed his fellow noblemen—and a fair share of noblewomen. But like all warriors of his age, he had also worn a sword and he certainly knew how to handle one. Takamura's martial skills had been passed down the generations and improved upon by his descendants who had settled in the province of Musashi and founded the Yokoyamadō. They had been perfected by the Narita, the Nara, the Beppu, and the Tamai, who had spent much of their life in the heat of battle. They, too, had fought with bow and arrow, but as the chroniclers of the *Hōgen monogatari* recorded so graphically, they were already equally adept at the use of the long sword. Ienaga had passed their facility with the sword and their techniques on to his own offspring, and given it the name by which it has survived into the century in which the three brothers had been born: the Chūjō-ryū, the school of fencing of the Chūjō clan. By that time, the sword had begun to overtake the bow as the warrior's weapon of choice, and the Chūjō-ryū had developed into a sophisticated school of swordsmanship, with its own distinct tech-

## Chūjō Hyōgo no Kami Nagahide

Swordsmen practice their skill, even on the corpses of the executed

niques and its own martial philosophy that had its roots in Confucian, Buddhist, and Shintō teachings.

As a warrior in a long line of warriors, and with much time on his hands, the crippled Kagenaga passed all his learning and martial skills on to his sons. One more child had been born to him, a boy whom he had named Tokinaga. Both boys were born during the 1330s, a time when the struggle between the Southern and Northern Courts was at its height, and no effort was spared by Kagenaga to inculcate in the young boys the mental and physical skills by which their ancestors had survived the challenges and turmoils of their own times. Being the eldest of the two, Nagahide was destined to follow in his father's footsteps, to preserve and develop his clan's wealth of martial knowledge and pass it on to the next generation.

Nagahide was a bright young man, a great lover of books, especially those containing the poets of his distant ancestor Ono Takamura. At the same time

# Famous Samurai: The Two Courts Period

*Opposite page*: The great Nitta Yoshisada, casting his sword into the sea at Cape Inamura

he was a good warrior, who applied his martial skills to the crushing of the Loyalists with a fierceness that even surprised his father. Having been born in the wake of the Kenmu Restoration, and into a family of Bakufu officials, the young Nagahide was raised in the belief that the Loyalists were rebels who needed to be crushed in order to preserve national stability and secure the future of his own family. Few could have foreseen at that time, least of all the young Nagahide himself, to what extent that rich and proud family tradition, tied so closely to the fortunes of the Bakufu, would become the bearer of a style of fencing that had been inspired by the Loyalist cause. It would be a meeting of minds that would come to challenge many of the certainties with which the young Nagahide had been raised, for the man who came to exert such an influence over the adult Nagahide and his style of fencing was none other than Nenami Jion, alias Sōma Yoshimoto, son of the great Loyalist hero Sōma Tadashige, the direct vassal of Nitta Yoshisada.

## Constable of Owari

Nagahide had been lucky. With the exception of Narita Moritsuna, all his ancestors had fought for the cause that had eventually prevailed. It had been so for Narita Sukehiro, when he had remained loyal to Minamoto Yoriyoshi, and it had been so for Chūjō Kagenaga, when he had remained loyal to Ashikaga Takauji. In a feudal age in which loyalty was the cohesive glue that held society together, such decisions were chiefly determined by existing family connections. Those connections, however, were complicated and diverse, and if a clan chieftain played his cards well he would have more than one option to choose from.

Building on the good fortune and successes of his ancestors, Nagahide was able to start out on his own career, and this he did with a considerable degree of good fortune as well as sound judgment. He inherited the family estate of Takahashi in 1354, shortly after his father had taken the tonsure. With that succession came the hereditary title of governor of Dewa province, not an important post but one with considerable status, as well as sentimental overtones, as it had first been held by his grandfather, Chūjō Yorihira.

Chūjō Hyōgo no Kami Nagahide

# Famous Samurai: The Two Courts Period

The bridge across the Yahagi River at Okazaki, a few miles downriver from Koromo

Yet it was not only privilege that propelled Nagahide into a position of influence. His cultured side earned him the first important post within the Bakufu bureaucracy. Experiences gained in helping his uncle with the construction and finance of temples and shrines within their own domain earned him his first important post, that of *jisha bugyō*, the magistrate in charge of temples and shrines, while his good judgment of people's characters that of *onshōgata*, the officer in charge of the distribution of military honors and rewards. Nor did his qualities as a governor go unrecognized by the Bakufu, who appointed him not only to constable of Owari province in succession to his father, but also that of Iga province, posts which he occupied during the 1350s, when he was in his early twenties. He reached the pinnacle of his impressive civil career within the ranks of the Bakufu during the following decade, when, like his father and many of his ancestors before him, he was appointed as a member of the Board of Councilors.

## Chūjō Hyōgo no Kami Nagahide

The occupation of such an important post required Nagahide to at least intermittently take up residency in Kamakura, still very much the military capital of Japan. It must have been somewhere in the course of 1366 that, during one of his protracted stays at Kamakura, the Bakufu administrator befriended a man who might well have been his enemy. Indeed, to all intents and purposes he did belong to the enemy camp, for the monk who befriended and introduced the Bakufu dignitary to a new style of swordsmanship was non other than Nenami Jion, the son of the murdered Loyalist warrior Sōma Tadashige, who in that year had entered the Jufuku temple to study the Japanese art of swordsmanship under the tutelage of Shinsō Eisuke.

## Meeting of Minds

It is not hard to conceive what brought Nagahide to the Jufuku temple. The Jufuku temple was as old as the Bakufu itself and was closely associated with Kamakura's martial culture. It had been founded by none other than Myōan Eisai, a Tendai monk who had been converted to Chan Buddhism on one of his pilgrimages to China. On his return, he had sought to convince the court of its merits, but the jealousy and belligerent interference of the existing sects had frustrated his attempts and forced him to decamp to Kamakura. There, he had soon found willing ears among the Hōjō leaders, who at that time were eagerly looking for a means by which they could evolve a culture that could rival that of the court in Kyoto. Chan Buddhism, or Zen as it came to be known in Japan, came to play an invaluable role in this endeavor. As in the past, when the Nara court had first turned their attention toward the Chinese mainland, the rich and variegated vehicle of the Buddhist faith, with all its accompanying, rites, rules, rituals, art, and artifacts, proved to be a perfect medium by which the latest developments in Chinese culture could be introduced and adapted to Bakufu requirements. One of these, of course, was the propagation of military ethics, and here, too, Zen Buddhism, with its emphasis on self-reliance and discipline, was perfectly suited to the tastes and sensibilities of the newly emerging warrior class, and proved a perfect tool in the hands of the Bakufu rulers. The new creed also brought learning

# Famous Samurai: The Two Courts Period

Kamakura's Jufuku temple, where Nagahide and Jion first met

and esteem to those who practiced it, and the Hōjō leaders were quick to capitalize on its potential to harness their position vis-a-vis the imperial court—a tradition that was gratefully continued by the Ashikaga leaders.

The encounter between the Bakufu administrator and the monk at the Jufuku temple was nevertheless a remarkable one, all the more so in that it was the first of many more encounters in which they exchanged their techniques and insights into each other's style of swordsmanship—a mutual interest that became the basis of a true and lasting friendship.

That friendship seemed at the same time natural and yet impossible. Both sons of warriors, both men of great intellectual depth, but one so tested by fate and the other so favored. It is simply inconceivable that the monk-turned fugitive would or even could have confided in his new-won friend, revealed his true identity, or even hinted to the true mission that lay behind his mastery of the sword. Divulging to Nagahide his hatred of Sōma

## Chūjō Hyōgo no Kami Nagahide

Chikatane, the Bakufu ally whose henchmen had murdered his father, would at best have been the end of their acquaintance. Any hint of his intention to assassinate Chikatane out of revenge for the death of his father would certainly have been the end of him, whether a monk or not. Nagahide, after all, was a member of the highest Bakufu organ and even the faintest suspicion that his friend might threaten the life of one of its members would have forced him to take action.

What was it then that brought these so divergent men together and caused such a deep and lasting friendship to develop between them in spite of their different allegiances? In material terms, at least, there was no incentive on either side, Nagahide because he did not need any, Jion because he did not want any—he was a monk with a monk's requirements and it is unlikely that he looked to Nagahide for any financial or other favors. Why then, would the monk have initiated the council member in the precepts of the Nen school of fencing to the degree he did? There can be only one answer to the mystery of their friendship and that must be their great mutual passion for the art of fencing.

While Jion was by far the greater swordsmen of the two, his talent was as yet a hidden one in that his fugitive life had prevented him from pursuing a life of *musha shugyō*, let alone openly propagate his particular school of fencing. He was forced to move from monastery to monastery, furtively, clad in the anonymous garb of a Buddhist priest and often under cover of the night, in constant fear as he must have been of being exposed as the son of a Loyalist hero. Never could he openly engage a great swordsman in a contest of strength, challenging him in the traditional way by proudly stating his name and pedigree and enumerating in elaborate detail his and his ancestor's martial feats. Physically he was a free man, but spiritually he was a man in shackles, bound as he was to preserve his true identity for the man who had so treacherously killed his father.

How much easier it was for Nagahide. His prominent position within the Bakufu and the great public exposure and esteem that came with it had enabled the swordsman to organize contests in which the Chūjō school of fencing took pride of place. In doing so, he was able to build on an ancient family tradition. All of his distant ancestors—the heroes who had featured largely

# Famous Samurai: The Two Courts Period

*Opposite page:*
Ashikaga Yoshimitsu, pupil of Chūjō Nagahide

in the tales of the Hōgen and Heiji disturbances, and the men who had fought hard in the Gempei War—all had been swordsmen of great repute. And while the techniques of his more immediate ancestors may have suffered from the relatively peaceful times in which they lived, the esteem that came with their high rank had sustained the reputation of the Chūjō-ryū where other schools of fencing had faded into obscurity. He was widely hailed as one of Japan's foremost swordsmen and became the fencing instructor of the third shogun of the Muromachi Bakufu, Ashikaga Yoshimitsu.

The most compelling proof of the enduring nature of their friendship came four decades after their first encounter, after the swordsman had once more retired from secular life to spend his last days in quiet meditation among the mountains of the Japanese Alps. It must have been sometime in the early 1390s that Jion left the comfort of his mountain retreat at Namiai, and set out on an arduous journey by foot across the mountain to the upstream village of Hiraya. From there he followed the river to Kamiyahagi, where he boarded the small boat of a fisherman and set off down the Yahagi River to seek out his old friend, then in retirement on his estate of Takahashi. By then the Bakufu and Loyalist troops had long since laid down their weapons and the Northern and Southern Courts had been unified, and it seems that the two men, the one prematurely aged by a life of turmoil, the other at the end of a distinguished but taxing career, had chosen to let bygones be bygones and forget the circumstances of fate that had put their fathers on opposite sides of the battlefield. Nagahide, on his part, must have weighed the wrongs and injustices that had driven the young warrior's son to assassinate an important Bakufu ally. Yet the leap of faith must have been greatest for the monk, as it was he who stood to lose the most by their renewed acquaintance. In avenging his father's death, custom had required the monk to resume his true name and thus discard the robe of secrecy he had worn for so long. It must have been a difficult choice for Jion to seek out his old friend and face the risk of persecution—a choice in which he must have been guided by his religious beliefs. In the end his courage was amply rewarded, for it is almost certain that the considerable funds for the construction of his temple were raised by none other than Chūjō Nagahide. Sadly, Nagahide never lived to see the temple completed. He died in 1384, an old

## Chūjō Hyōgo no Kami Nagahide

man at piece with the world. Yet the proof of the monk's gratitude toward his friend and benefactor was there for all who cared to read it; it lay in the very name of the temple he founded, for when it was completed Jion took the Chinese reading of the first character, naga, of Nagahide and used its Chinese reading, chō, to name his temple Chōfukuji.

# Heritage

The reacquaintance between the two old friends did not merely culminate in the founding of the Chōfuku temple. Though their friendship was built on mutual respect, there was a constructive imbalance in both men's intellectual and physical talents. In the realm of politics and scholastics, it was Nagahide who exceeded his friend by far. His profound knowledge of law, administration, Chinese philosophy, and literature in general made him in many ways a teacher to the man who had been forced to flee his home at the age of five and abandon his prospects for the kind of education Nagahide had enjoyed. Yet monastic life had given Jion a means to make up for his lack of learning, and it had given him the unsurpassed martial skills that had given his life meaning and direction. And it was here, in the realm of fencing, that Jion was Nagahide's master.

In the course of almost half a century Jion had absorbed the influences of many different schools of fencing—the crude fencing skills of the *sōhei* at the Yugyō monastery, the exotic mainland techniques of the Chinese mercenary at the Anba temple, the traditional Japanese style of fencing of Shinsō Eisuke at the Jufuku temple, the unembellished cuts and thrusts of the battlefield during his stay at the Dazaifu Tenmangu, and the finesses of dueling, an art he had acquired during his long years of *musha shugyō*. All these divergent, at times even conflicting, influences, he had gathered into a vast and bewildering array of *kata*, fixed sequences of movements used to practice and pass on a specific fencing technique to the next generation. It is believed that, by the time he had settled in Namiai, the warrior-monk had to his disposal close to a hundred techniques, many of them variations on the same theme, developed to meet the conditions that might arise in the heat of battle

A pillar still marks the site of Koromo (also Kanaya) castle

or in a two-man contest. Only his closest pupils ever managed to master all these techniques, yet not even they could have completely grasped their various nuances or fathom the deeper insights of his eclectic learning. Consequently, a great part of Jion's knowledge had been lost to posterity forever; parts of certain techniques were absorbed into the techniques of other schools while other parts simply went out of use, as their specific use and context were lost on a new generation.

It is to Chūjō Nagahide's great credit that Jion's impressive heritage has been preserved to this very day. During his last years the two swordsmen saw a lot of each other. Being the younger of the two, Jion would visit Koromo castle several times a year and spend several weeks as Nagahide's guest.

# Famous Samurai: The Two Courts Period

The majestic Yahagi River

During those weeks, which must have been some of the happiest of his life, the two men would indulge in the pastimes of warriors: playing a game of *shōgi*, and composing poetry over a cup of sake. Or they might take a boat up the Yahagi River. Most of their time, however, they spent in the pursuit of their chief passion: the art of fencing. By now they were old men, slowed down by the limitations of old men's physiques and their practice must have been chiefly one of going through the paces and the careful analysis of sequences. Yet their age also brought its advantages. They were men at ease with themselves, free from the urge to prove their mettle, and eager to pass on to the next generation the knowledge acquired in a lifetime of martial pursuits. The survival of their intellectual heritage beyond the grave—to see it live on where they must inevitably die—was now their main concern.

In this respect Jion's Nen-ryū posed the greatest hurdle. It was the heritage of a man in whose hands it had been at the same time a tool of deadly

## Chūjō Hyōgo no Kami Nagahide

precision, a technique of great sophistication, and an art of dazzling beauty—a school, in short, superior to most of the crude arts of swordsmanship practiced in his day. Ultimately, however, the Nen-ryū was the creation of just one man, however gifted; it had not gone through the evolutionary process that made other schools, such as the Chūkō-ryū, a pliable tool in the hands of the next generation. It was simply too complicated, too much weighed down by the idiosyncrasies of a man who had led an exemplary but singular life, and its teachings too esoteric to be comprehended by even the most devoted of disciples. And it was here that Nagahide, with his great talent for organization, played an invaluable role. Sadly, no records directly from Nagahide's hands have survived, but those drafted by his immediate successors openly praise his contribution and still bear the imprint of his rigorous mind. Nagahide arranged the great plethora of techniques, exercises, and movements into a well-organized group of thirty-three distinct *kata*, each containing the carefully distilled essence of techniques that were determined by a given context and employed toward a stated aim.

The Chūjō-ryū was not the only school of fencing to be influenced by Jion's teachings. But due to their prominent position within the Muromachi Bakufu, Nagahide's descendants became the main lineage through which Jion's style of fencing was transmitted down the generations. For six generations Jion's teachings were passed on by the Chūjō clan from father to son, apparently without spawning any major new styles, until, toward the end of the sixteenth century, one of its practitioners, a man by the name of Kanemaki Jisai, met with another towering figure in the landscape of Japanese martial arts. This was Itō Ittōsai, the swordsman who was to use the Chūjō-ryū—and thus a substantial part of Jion's heritage—as the basis for one of the major swordsmanship schools of the Edo Period, the famous Ittō-ryū, or "single-sword" school of fencing.

Chūjō Nagahide has gone down in history as a paragon of the *bunbu no tassha*, a man accomplished in the civil and military arts. He was a man of wide learning and great administrative abilities, who during his term in office made considerable contributions to the prosperity of his country under the rule of the Muromachi Bakufu. Like his remote ancestor Ono Takamura, he was also a gifted poet, whose writings have survived the ravages of time in

# Famous Samurai: The Two Courts Period

works such as the *Chokusen wakashū*, an anthology of Japanese poetry whose first edition was compiled under the auspices of Emperor Go-Daigo. It is hard to say in which of the many fields of human endeavor in which he was at home Nagahide (whose name was made up of the character for "long" and "excellence") excelled the most, yet to many a swordsman, both in the past and the present, his contribution to the art of Japanese swordsmanship is his greatest legacy. It is a testimony to a civilization in which such emphasis was put on a balanced development of one's civil as well as one's martial accomplishments, that Nagahide achieved fame through his mastery of both.

Chūjō Hyōgo no Kami Nagahide

# Principal characters in this chapter

| | |
|---|---|
| Akushichi Bettō: | The elder brother of Minamoto Tametomo, and one of the warriors from Musashi to play an active part in the Hōgen Rebellion. |
| Chiba Hirotsune: | Vice governor of Kazusa, who joined the camp of Go-Shirakawa during the Hōgen Rebellion. |
| Chiba Tsunetane: | Vice governor of Shimōsa, who joined the camp of Go-Shirakawa during the Hōgen Rebellion. |
| Chūjō Hidenaga: | Third son of Chūjō Yorihira, and successor to his father, Chūjō Yorihira. |
| Chūjō Ienaga: | Inheritor of Narita Moritsuna's estate and founder of the Chūjō clan. |
| Chūjō Kagenaga: | Father of Chūjō Nagahide, and Governor of Dewa, who was wounded in battle at the Yahagi River. |
| Chūjō Nagamune: | Governor of Izu and son of Chūjō Yorihira. |
| Chūjō Tokinaga: | Brother of Chūjō Nagahide. |
| Chūjō Yorihira: | Constable of Owari province, and grandfather of Chūjō Nagahide. |
| Fujiwara Nobuyori: | Disaffected court noble who sought to overthrow Taira Kiyomori with Minamoto Yoshitomo's help in the Heiji Rebellion. |
| Fujiwara Tsunemitsu: | Governor of Musashi and founder of the Chūjō clan. |
| Fujiwara Tsunetsugu: | Leader of the last Heian mission to China. |
| Fujiwara Yorinaga: | Heian courtier who joined the faction of Sutoku and was killed in the Hōgen Rebellion. |
| Go-Shirakawa: | Emperor and rival of Sutoku in the Hōgen Rebellion. |
| Hatta Tomoie: | Adoptive father of Chūjō Ienaga, and founder of the Oda clan. |
| Hōjō Tokimasa: | Governor of Izu, who acted as guardian of the young Minamoto Yoritomo. |
| Hōjō Tokimasa: | First Hōjō leader to assume the post of *shikken* to |

# Famous Samurai: The Two Courts Period

| | |
|---|---|
| | the infant Minamoto Yoriie and become the de facto leader of the Kamakura Bakufu. |
| Ike no Zen'ni: | Mother of Taira Yorimori, who pleaded with her stepson, Tarai Kiyomori, to save the life of the young captive Minamoto Yoritomo. |
| Minamoto Tametomo: | Eight son of Minamoto Tameyoshi, who warned Taira Fujiwara Yorinaga of the pending attack. |
| Minamoto Tameyoshi: | Minamoto chieftain who joined the camp of Sutoku with six of his sons during the Hōgen Rebellion. |
| Minamoto Tomonaga: | Second son of Minamoto Yoshitomo, wounded at Ryūge pass and killed by his father to keep him from falling into the hands of Taira Kiyomori's henchmen. |
| Minamoto Tsunetomo: | Minamoto chieftain who brought the rebel Taira Masakado to heel. |
| Minamoto Yoriie: | Son of Minamoto Yoritomo, whose wild nature made him unfit to lead the Bakufu. |
| Minamoto Yorimasa: | The only son of Minamoto Tameyoshi to join the faction of emperor Go-Shirakawa during the Hōgen Rebellion. |
| Minamoto Yorinobu: | Minamoto chieftain who brought the rebel Taira Tadatsune to heel. |
| Minamoto Yoritomo: | Third son of Minamoto Yoshitomo, who survived the Heiji Rebellion to overthrow the Taira in the Gempei War and found the Kamakura Bakufu. |
| Minamoto Yoriyoshi: | Minamoto chieftain, sent to the northern provinces by the Heian court to suppress the Emishi. |
| Minamoto Yoshichika: | Governor of Tsushima island, who became notorious through his misrule. |
| Minamoto Yoshihira: | Eldest son of Minamoto Yoshitomi, whose advice Nobuyori to ambush Taira Kiyomori on his return from Kumano was turned down by Fujiwara Nobuyori. |

| | |
|---|---|
| Minamoto Yoshiie: | Minamoto chieftain, and great hero of the northern campaigns. |
| Minamoto Yoshitomo: | Eldest son of Minamoto Tameyoshi, and the only one to join the faction of Go-Shirakawa in the Hōgen Rebellion, and who was killed by one of Taira Kiyomori's henchmen during his flight following the Heiji Rebellion. |
| Narita Moritsuna: | One of the few members of the Narita clan to serve in the imperial troops, and who lost his life during the Jōkyū rebellion. |
| Narita Sukehiro: | (Narita no Tarō) Eldest son of Narita Suketaka, and one of the warriors from Musashi to play an active part in the Hōgen Rebellion. |
| Narita Suketaka: | Son of Ono Yoshitaka and founder of the Narita clan, and also known as Narita no Taifū. |
| Nijō: | Go-Shirakawa's son, who defected to the camp of Taira Kiyomori during the Heiji Rebellion. |
| Ōgo Shigetoshi: | Chieftain from the province of Kōzuke, who joined Minamoto Yoshitomo in the Heiji Rebellion. |
| Okabe Tadanori: | Member of the Musashi Nanadō, who joined Minamoto Yoshitomo in the Heiji Rebellion. |
| Ono Suketaka: | Son of Yoshitaka, and founder of the Narita clan. |
| Ono Takamura: | Heian court noble, and Chūjō Nagahide's distant ancestor. |
| Ono Takayasu: | Descendant of Ono Takamura, and governor of Musashi. |
| Ono Yoshitaka: | Son of Ono Yoshiyasu, third governor of Musashi, and founder of the Yoko-yamadō. |
| Ono Yoshiyasu: | Son of Ono Takayasu and second governor of Musashi. |
| Osada Tadamune : | Father-in-law of Kamada Masakiyo who went over to the side of the Taira and assassinated Minamoto Yoshitomo during his flight from the capital. |

# Famous Samurai: The Two Courts Period

| | |
|---|---|
| Saitō Bettō Sanemori: | One of the warriors from Musashi to play an active part in the Hōgen Rebellion. |
| Shinzei: | Monk and friend of Taira Kiyomori, who died in Heiji Rebellion. |
| Shirakawa: | Emperor of the Heian court. |
| Sutoku: | Retired emperor and rival of Go-Shirakawa during the Hōgen Rebellion. |
| Taira Iesada: | Taira chieftain from Iga, with whose help Taira Kiyomori was able to safely return to Rokuhara from his pilgrimage to Kumano. |
| Taira Kiyomori: | Son of Taira Tadamori and clan chieftain during the Hōgen Rebellion, in which he joined the faction of Go-Shirakawa. |
| Taira Korehira: | Governor of Ise and founder of the Ise Taira. |
| Taira Masakado: | Rebel from Shimōsa province, who sought to overthrow the central government. |
| Taira Masamori: | Governor of Inaba, appointed by the Heian court to bring Minamoto Yoshichika to heel. |
| Taira Shigemori: | Son of Taira Kiyomori and commander who led the assault on the imperial palace following Nijō's defection. |
| Taira Tadamasa: | Uncle of Taira Kiyomori, who was murdered by the latter for taking the side of the Sutoku faction in the Hōgen and Heiji Rebellions. |
| Taira Tadamori: | Son of Taira Sadamori, who increased his clan's influence over the Heian court. |
| Taira Yorimori: | Governor of Owari province, who captured Minamoto Yoritomo on his flight from the capital. |
| Tama-i Shirō: | Fourth son of Narita Suketaka, and one of the warriors from Musashi to join Minamoto Yoshitomo in the Heiji Rebellion. |

# GLOSSARY

*akusō*: Militant monks belonging to rival Buddhist sects, and the precursor of the notorious *sōhei*.

*bunbu no tassha*: Man accomplished in the civil and military arts.

*bunbu ryōdō*: The dual way of learning and fighting.

*gokenin*:: Direct retainers of the shogun.

*jisha bugyō*: Bakufu official in charge of temples and shrines.

*kata*: Sequence of movements used to practice and to pass on a fencing technique to the next generation.

*mukaijō*: Makeshift stronghold built facing existing strongholds to isolated it from others.

*musha shugyō*: Literally, "warrior training," the practice of ascetic self-discipline that goes back to the ancient traditions of the mysterious *yamabushi*, or mountain monks.

*naginata*: Pole sword.

*nairan*: Assistant to an emperor with governmental powers.

*okugi*: Innermost secrets of an art or craft.

*onshōgata*: Bakufu official in charge of the distribution of military honors.

*rōnin*: Masterless samurai.

*seki*: "Barrier," or border post, where taxes are levied and by which movement between provinces was controlled.

*shikken*: Regent to the infant shogun.

# Famous Samurai: The Two Courts Period

| | |
|---|---|
| *sōhei*: | Warrior monks of the great Buddhist temples. |
| *taryū shiai*: | Literally, "contest of different schools," and used to refer to a duel between two swordsmen. |
| *tatsujin*: | Person who has reached a high level of attainment in a field of learning or of art. |
| *tsuitōshi*: | General of punitive expedition for quelling a revolt. |
| *yamabushi*: | Reclusive mountain monks of the Japanese Alps, who practiced austerities in the harsh environment of the mountains in order to attain holy or super-human powers. |
| *yari*: | Spear or lance. |

# INDEX

Akamatsu Norimura 17, 18
Anba temple 52, 54–57
Ashikaga Tadayoshi 12, 14, 19
Ashikaga Takauji 12, 14–20, 22–23, 26, 28, 30, 41, 57, 61, 64, 143
Ashikaga Yoshimitsu 64

**B**
Beppu no Jirō 114

**C**
Chiba Hirotsune 114, 129
Chiba Sadatane 10
Chiba Tsunetane 114
Chōfuku temple 70–71
Chōkō temple 145
*Chokusen wakashū* 160
Chūjō Hidenaga 142, 144
Chūjō Ienaga 140, 141–42
Chūjō Kagenaga 142–44, 147
Chūjō Nagahide 80, 87
Chūjō Nagamune 142
Chūjō Shingo 114
Chūjō Tokinaga 147

Chūjō Tsunemitsu 129, 141
Chūjō Tsunetaka 142
Chūjō Yorihira 142
Chūjō-ryū 146

**D**
Daigo, Emperor (885–930) 61
Date Yukitomo 38, 40
Dazaifu 59, 63, 65

**E**
Eda Yukiyoshi 18
Eifuku monastery 14
Enryaku temple 15, 51

**F**
Fuchū castle 32–33
Fujigatani castle 1, 2, 41
Fujishima castle 35–36
Fujishima shrine 35
Fujiwara Kamatari 90
Fujiwara Michinori. See Shinzei
Fujiwara Nobuyori 119, 121–22, 125
Fujiwara Tsunemitsu 90

# Famous Samurai: The Two Courts Period

Fujiwara Tsunetsugu 82
Fujiwara Yorinaga 109

**G**

Go-Daigo, Empeor (1288–1339) 4, 5, 7, 12–24, 32, 42, 143
Go-Sanjō (1034–1073) 108
Go-Shirakawa, Emperor (1034–73) 108–12, 115, 120–27, 135, 136
Go-Toba, Emperor (1180–1239) 136–38
Gokuraku temple 10–11
*Goseibai shikimoku* 141

**H**

Hakota no Jirō 114
Hatta Tomoie 138–39
*Heiji monogatari* 122
*Heike monogatari* 104
Heisen temple 51
Higuchi Kaneshige 73
Hiyoriyama castle 45
*Hōgen monogatari* 114, 129, 146
Hōjō Moritoki 11
Hōjō Sadamasa 10
Hōjō Takatoki 5, 7, 12
Hōjō Tokimasa 132, 133, 137–38
Hōjō Yasuie 8–10
Hōjō Yasutoki 137, 140
Honma Magojirō 24
Horiguchi Sadamitsu 7
Hōryū monastery 82
Hosokawa Takamoto 36

**I**

Ikushina shrine 7
Imagawa Sadayo 60
Imagawa Tadaaki 62
Imagawa Yoshinori 62

Ishibashi Kazuyoshi 18
Ishido Yoshifusa 38, 41–42
Ittō-ryū 73
Iwagami no Tarō 114

**J**

*Jinnō shōtōki* 42
Jōkō monastery 140
Jōkōmyō temple 14
Jufuku temple 59, 66

**K**

Kakusa Kimisuke 36
Kamada Masakiyo 129
Kanagasaki castle 26, 28–29, 31
Kanayama castle 4
Kanegasaki castle 32
Kaneyoshi 63
Kazan palace 4
Kehi Ujiharu 26, 30
Kitabatake Akiie 15–17, 40–42
Kitabatake Akinobu 45
Kitabatake Chikafusa 15, 42–44, 47, 59, 140
Kō Morofuyu 44, 46
Kō Moroyasu 14, 27, 44
Kōfuku monastery 112
Koma castle 44
Kōmyō, Emperor (1321–80) 23
Konoe, Emperor (1139–55) 109
Kuromaru castle 33, 35–36
Kusunoki Masashige 17, 21

**M**

Minamoto Tadamasa 110, 116
Minamoto Tametomo 112–13–17
Minamoto Tameyoshi 104, 110, 116, 118

# Index

Minamoto Tomonaga 127–28
Minamoto Yoriie 137
Minamoto Yorimasa 110
Minamoto Yorinobu 101, 114
Minamoto Yoritomo 2, 127, 131–32, 134–36, 139
Minamoto Yoriyoshi 92, 148
Minamoto Yoshichika 97, 100–102
Minamoto Yoshihira 123, 125, 128, 131
Minamoto Yoshiie 96–97, 99–100, 110, 118
Minamoto Yoshikuni 110
Minamoto Yoshitomo 66, 110, 113, 115, 117, 120–27, 129, 131, 139
Minamoto Yoshitsune 135
Minamoto Yoshiyasu 110
Mitsuishi castle 18–19
Morinaga, Crown Prince (1308–35) 42

## N

Nagasaki Takashige 8
Nakano Fujiuchisaemon 36
Nara no Saburō 114
Narita Moritsuna 135–37, 148
Narita no Tarō 114
Narita Suketaka 92, 129
Narita Suketsuna 135
Narita Sukezane 131
Narita Takanaga 129
Narita Yoshisuke 137
Narita Yukitaka 129
Nen-ryū 74
Nijō, Emperor (1143–65) 120, 125
Nitta Yoshiaki 32
Nitta Yoshisada 2, 4, 7–8, 10–11, 15–23, 27–28, 30–32, 35–38, 41, 47, 143, 148

## O

Oda castle 40, 42, 44, 139
Oda Haruhisa 40, 139
Oda Nobunaga 51, 142
Ōdachi Muneuji 7
Odaka castle 41
Ōgo Shigetoshi 129
Ono Imoko 82
Ono shrine 86–87
Ono Suketaka 89
Ono Takamura 79–82, 84, 146–47
Ono Takayasu 84, 86–87, 89
Ono Yoshitaka 87, 89
Ooida Ujitsune 18–19
Osada Tadamune 129
Oyama castle 40
Oyama Datakaie 40
Oyama Hidetomo 10

## R

Ryōzan castle 38

## S

Saitō Sanemori 115
Sakurada Sadakuni 8
Sanage shrine 145
Sanjūsangendō 106
Satomi 31
Satomi Yoshitane 7
Satomi Yoshiuji 29
Seki castle 41, 44–47
Seki Munesuke 41, 47
Shiba Ienaga 19, 26
Shiba Takatsune 24, 26, 32–33, 35–36
Shigehito, Emperor 109
Shimotsuma Masayasu 46, 47
*Shin kokinshū* 80
Shinsō Eisuke 58, 66

169

# Famous Samurai: The Two Courts Period

Shinzei 121–22
Shinzenkōji castle 28
Shirakawa, Emperor (1053–1129) 100, 107
Shirakawa castle 43
Shirohata castle 18–19
Sōma Chikatane 41, 49, 65
Sōma Tadashige 1, 2, 7, 23–24, 38–39, 41, 47–48, 65, 73, 148
Sōma Tanemochi 48
Sōma Yoshikado 1
Sōma Yoshimoto 1
Somoyama castle 28, 30–33, 38–39
Sugawara Michizane 59–60
Sun Tzu 91
Sutoku, Emperor (1119–64) 109, 113

**T**
Taga castle 16, 38, 42, 45
*Taiheiki* 7, 23, 29, 92
Taihō castle 45, 46
Taira Masakado's 87
Taira Kiyomori 106, 107, 108, 109, 110, 113, 116, 117, 118, 121, 122, 123, 124, 125, 129, 132
Taira Korehira 95
Taira Masakado 101
Taira Masamori 99, 101, 102, 103, 104
Taira Motomori 110
Taira no Masakado 1
Taira Shigemori 125
Taira Tadamori 104, 106, 119, 132
Taira Tadatsune 114
Taira Yorimori 132
*Takamura monogatari* 80
Takanaga 24, 30
Takasaki castle 62
Tamai no Shirō 114
*The Art of War* 91
Toba, Emperor (1103–56) 104
Tōdai temple 95
Tokugawa Ieyasu 80
Tōshō monastery 12
Tsunenaga, Crown Prince (1324–38) 24, 30
Tsutsumi Takarayama 73

**U**
Uryū Tamotsu 26, 28, 29, 31
Utsunomiya castle 40
Utsunomiya Kintsuna 40

**W**
Wakiya Yoshiharu 31
Wakiya Yoshisuke 7, 18, 19, 24, 28, 31, 33

**Y**
Yamaki Kanetaka 133
Yorinaga 110, 113
Yugyō monastery 49, 50, 52, 68
Yūki Chikatomo 42, 43, 44
Yūki Munehiro 38, 42

TOYO Press publishes books that contribute to a deeper understanding of Asian cultures. Editorial supervision: Ray Furse. Book and cover design: Chōkei Studios. Printing and binding: IngramSpark. The typefaces used are Purloin, Futurist, Herculanum, and Prescript.

www.ingramcontent.com/pod-product-compliance
Lightning Source LLC
Chambersburg PA
CBHW042035100526

44587CB00030B/4429